Fireside Stories

FIRESIDE STORIES

Heartwarming Tales of Life, Love, and Laughter

WRITTEN AND COMPILED BY

MARY HOLLINGSWORTH

WORD PUBLISHING

NASHVILLE

A Thomas Nelson Company

Other Books by
Mary Hollingsworth

A Few Hallelujahs for Your Ho Hums
Apple Blossoms
The Divorce Recovery Guide
For Mom with Love
The Grief Adjustment Guide
Help! I Need a Bulletin Board
Hugs for Kids
Hugs for Women
It's a One-derful Life!
Just Between Friends
Living Lights, Shining Stars
On Raising Children
Rainbows
Speaking of Love
Together Forever
and more than fifty books for children,
including these:
My Little Bible
The International Children's Story Bible
Just Imagine with Barney the Dinosaur
The Kids-Life Bible Storybook

*W*ith love to my brother,
Frank Shrode,
who shares my enjoyment of a great story
and the class of a well-printed page

Contents

∼✐ Contents ✐∼

CONTENTS

CONTENTS

Preface

Stories are the essence of life. They are the golden nuggets left in the bottom of the pan when the dirt has been washed away. They are the part of life that's remembered and treasured—the gem worth keeping.

Stories are forever tales. They are told over and again down through the ages, from generation to generation, because we want to keep the adventures and the people alive, in our memories if not in our realities. They preserve our faith, our traditions, our histories, and our fantasies.

Stories let us look at ourselves through the struggles and victories of others, like the great stories of the Bible. They say to us, "If *they* could overcome *their* problems, then, with God's help, *we* can overcome *our* problems." They give us hope and help and trust in the God who controls ultimate outcomes of life.

As a writer, stories are my stock in trade. Without stories, anecdotes, and illustrations, I'm just a typist, a boring lecturer, a fact repeater. It's the stories that bring information to life, give it heart and soul, apply it to everyday living, and make it useful. Stories allow words to breathe and leap and dance. Without them, words are just ink on paper—flat, one-dimensional, and dead.

Fireside Stories is a collection of some of my favorite stories and illustrations, both from my own experience and from the writings of great storytellers like Charles Swindoll, Barbara Johnson, Max Lucado, Tony Campolo, my dad, and others. Many of these stories are true, with some of the names changed to protect the people's privacy; some are fictional. Most of these stories are attributable to specific writers; others are newly written but based on facts from the public record or history and, therefore, have no attribution. Some are serious and sad; some are funny or joyful. All of them will touch your heart.

Join me now for a ride on the magic carpet called Story that carries us into other lands and times where heroes and villains are everyday people like you and me. And I pray that you find yourself laughing with delight or crying in empathy, as I did, at every turning page.

———

Mary Hollingsworth

Acknowledgments

$\mathcal{H}$*eartfelt thanks to my friends and family at Word Publishing,* who consistently make excellent, life-changing books possible. Each of you, regardless of your individual role, is a vital part of the process. Thanks for what you do daily to bring good news to the world in print. You're the best!

Humble thanks to the authors whose writings are included here. As Charles H. Spurgeon said, "I think all originality and no plagiarism makes for dull preaching" . . . and writing.

Special thanks to Charlotte Greeson, my dear friend, for invaluable research in locating stories for the book and for your constant support and encouragement in my work and life. I'm so grateful that God appointed us to be friends.

Thanks to my mom, who took turns with me making up stories and telling them when I was a preschooler. You set me on the exciting road of imagination and my career as a storyteller.

Thanks to my dad, who is known as the local storyteller among his friends and family, for teaching me how to make the most of a good story or joke.

And thanks to these other friends, without whom I could not have completed this joyful task: Paula Stiger, Carol Bartley, Vicki Graham, Rhonda Hogan, and Nancy Norris. Blessings and joy!

This is my story;

This is my song—

Praising my Savior

All the day long.

—

Fanny J. Crosby
"Blessed Assurance"

Abducted!

$\mathcal{M}$ichael Kit Demcheshen, a Ukrainian boy of fourteen, lived in Suhodol, Poland, when World War II broke out. He was one of six children in a family living in a small, out-of-the-way village. While his family was poor, they had great love for each other and were very close. They worked together, they played together, and they stayed together.

In July 1942, Michael was suddenly abducted from his home by the German Civil Authority and put on a private farm in Austria to work. He remained there in servitude until the war was over in May 1945. Then he spent two years in various displaced-persons camps in Austria, mostly working for English military motor pools.

Michael had no contact with his family after their letters stopped coming in 1944. He tried to contact them but without success. He concluded that all had most likely been lost during the war.

So in 1947, through the International Refugee Organization, he applied for immigration to Venezuela, South America. He was taken to Germany where he spent six weeks waiting for a boat to Venezuela.

Alone at age nineteen, Michael spent two years in Caracas working to survive in a foreign country where the language and customs were strange to him. It was in Caracas that he met Ledford and Mildred Hubbard, an American couple temporarily living in Venezuela. He became like a son to the Hubbards, and they were like parents to him. So the Hubbards decided to try and help Michael. When they returned to the United States, they made arrangements for Michael to come and stay with them.

On November 16, 1949, at age twenty-one, Michael came to the United States on a student visa and began attending college. Four years later, on June 20, 1953, he married Violet Baxter. In March 1954 Michael was granted permanent residence in the States, and on September 8, 1955, he became a United States citizen.

Michael and Violet worked and raised their happy family through the years. Eventually they retired in Okmulgee, Oklahoma, where they are still living.

In the early fall of 1996, a young Ukrainian girl came to the States as an exchange student to go to college. She was living in Wellston, Oklahoma, with a family who knew Michael and Violet. Michael and the girl talked about the Ukraine, and Michael told her his life story.

The girl's father is a professional musician in the Ukraine and travels to towns and villages entertaining the people. Michael asked her, when she wrote to her father, to ask him to check if any people named Demcheshen still lived in

Suhodol the next time he was there. And he gave her his parents' and brothers' and sisters' names.

In October 1996 a letter came from the girl's father. He had found all of Michael's family alive and well in the city of Lviv, about thirty-six kilometers from Suhodol. Michael's younger sister still lives in the old family house. Although Michael's parents are deceased, he has discovered his five original siblings and three more he had never known because they were born after he was taken away. He has also found dozens of nieces and nephews he had never met. In all there are about eighty Demcheshens in Suhodol and Lviv! His oldest sister, Martha, lives in Poland.

On November 4, 1996, after fifty-four years of believing his entire family was dead, and they believing that *he* was dead, Michael talked to one of his nephews—a doctor in Lviv. Although he struggled with the little-used language of his youth, the telephone reunion was wonderful. A few days later he talked to his sister (the doctor's mother).

In March of 1997, Michael flew to Lviv. He was met at the airport by thirty-eight relatives. Even though he didn't recognize any of them immediately, it was a sweet reunion indeed. With God's blessing, this boy who was abducted from his home now has his long-lost family back.

———

Michael Demcheshen

Correction, Please...

$\mathcal{I}$n the newspaper of a large northern city, the following small article reportedly appeared:

NOTICE FROM AERO PUBLISHING: To those of you who bought our book, *Skydiving Made Easy*, please enter the following correction on page 12, paragraph 3, line 2: The words "state zip code" should say "pull rip cord."

The notice went on to say, "We regret any inconvenience this mistake may have caused you. . . ."

I'll Take the Foot

$\mathcal{B}$efore supper began I suggested to Curtis (who was six) that he should serve Charissa (who was four) before he served himself. Naturally he wondered why, since the platter of chicken sat directly in front of him . . . and he was as hungry as a lion. I explained it is polite for fellas to serve girls before they serve themselves. The rule sounded weird, but he was willing . . . as long as she didn't take too long.

Well, you'd never guess what occurred. After prayer, he picked up the huge platter, held it for his sister, and asked which piece of chicken she wanted.

She relished all this attention. Being quite young, however, she had no idea which piece to take. So, very seriously, she replied, "I'd like the foot."

He glanced in my direction, frowned as the hunger pains shot through his stomach, then looked at her and said, "Uh . . . Charissa, Mother doesn't cook the foot!"

To which she replied, "Where is it?"

With increased anxiety he answered (a bit louder), "I don't know! The foot is somewhere else, not on this platter. Look, choose a piece. Hurry up."

She studied the platter and said, "Okay, just give me the hand."

By now their mother and I were biting our lips to refrain from laughing out loud. We would have intervened but decided to let them work it out alone. That's part of the training process.

"A chicken doesn't have a hand; it has a wing, Charissa."

"I hate the wing, Curtis . . . Oh, go ahead and give me the head."

By then I was headed for the bathroom. I couldn't hold my laughter any longer. Curtis was totally beside himself. His sister was totally frustrated, not being able to get the piece she wanted.

Realizing his irritation with her and the absence of a foot or hand or head, she finally said in an exasperated tone, "Oh, all right! I'll take the belly button!"

That did it. He reached in, grabbed a piece, and said, "That's the best I can do!" He gave her the breast, which was about as close to the belly button as he could get.

———

Charles R. Swindoll

Come Before Winter

A Little Tact

Tact is one of the lost arts of the twentieth century, isn't it? I heard about a man who lacked tact. He was the type of person who just couldn't say anything graciously. He and his wife owned a poodle. They loved this dog. It was the object of their affection. The wife was to take a trip abroad, and the first day away she made it to New York.

She called home and asked her husband, "How are things?"

He said, "The dog's dead!"

She was devastated.

After collecting her thoughts, she asked, "Why do you do that? Why can't you be more tactful?"

He said, "Well, what do you want me to say? The dog died."

She said, "Well, you can give it to me in stages. For example, you could say when I call you from New York, 'The dog is on the roof.' And then when I travel to London the next day and call, you could tell me, 'Honey, the dog fell off the roof.' And when I call you from Paris, you could add, 'Honey, the dog had to be taken to the vet. In fact, he's in the hospital, not doing well.' And finally, when I call you from Rome, 'Honey, brace yourself. Our dog died.' I could handle that."

The husband paused and said, "Oh, I see."

Then she asked, "By the way, how's Mother?"

And he said, "She's on the roof."

————

Michael LeBoeuf

How to Win Customers and Keep Them for Life

No, Not One

✢

*L*ittle Chad was a shy, quiet young fella. One day he came home and told his mother he'd like to make a valentine for everyone in his class. Her heart sank. She thought, *I wish he wouldn't do that!* because she had watched the children when they walked home from school. Her Chad was always behind them. They laughed and hung on to each other and talked to each other. But Chad was never included. Nevertheless, she decided she would go along with her son. So she purchased the paper and glue and crayons. For three whole weeks, night after night, Chad painstakingly made thirty-five valentines.

Valentine Day dawned, and Chad was beside himself with excitement! He carefully stacked the valentines up, put them in a bag, and bolted out the door. His mom decided to bake him his favorite cookies and serve them up warm and nice with a cool glass of milk when he came home from school. She just knew he'd be disappointed; maybe the cookies would ease the pain a little. It hurt her to think that he wouldn't get many valentines—maybe none at all.

That afternoon she had the cookies and milk out on the

table. When she heard the children outside, she looked out the window. Sure enough, here they came, laughing and having the best time. And, as always, there was Chad in the rear. He walked a little faster than usual. She fully expected him to burst into tears as soon as he got inside. His arms were empty, she noticed, and when the door opened she choked back the tears.

"Mommy has some warm cookies and milk for you."

But he hardly heard her words. He just marched right on by, his face aglow, and all he could say was, "Not a one . . . not a one."

Her heart sank.

And then he added, "I didn't forget a one, not a single one!"

Dale Galloway
Rebuild Your Life

The Amazing Little Room
✝

A country family came to the city to a big farm-machinery convention and arrived at a fancy hotel. The old mother waited in the car while the father and son went into the hotel lobby to register.

While in the lobby, the father and son saw some doors slide open, and an ugly old lady walking with a cane stepped into a tiny little room. The doors to the little room closed, then some lights blinked and bells rang. About two minutes later, the lights blinked again, and the bells rang. Suddenly the doors to the little room slid open and out stepped a gorgeous young woman who smiled brilliantly at them as she walked through the lobby and out the door.

Wide-eyed, the father turned to the son and said, "Son, quick, go get your mother!"

Rags and Grandmother

W̶hen I was a tiny girl, before I started to school, my older brother and I begged my dad to get us a dog. For several months he held out, not willing to add another mouth to feed to our already stretched-to-the-limit minister's budget.

One day the phone rang, and my dad answered. It was a veterinarian friend of his, who said, "Clyde, I've got a dog over here I think you'd like. Why don't you come over and see her?"

That was the day we got Rags—a white-and-black, wire-haired terrier with bushy eyebrows, long toenails, and just a black patch of hair where a tail should have been. She was an extremely bright, affectionate mama dog that immediately moved into our home and our hearts. Because she had no tail, when she wagged, she wagged all over.

Rags soon learned to howl in tune to my brother's clarinet, tiptoe into the house at night so my dad couldn't hear her, and catch popcorn in midair. She was a great watchdog, a fun playmate, and a good friend to everyone in the neighborhood, except the cats. She hated cats with good, old-fashioned canine passion. She was everything a family pet was supposed to be.

When I was in the third grade, my folks decided to become houseparents at a children's home a few miles away. The only problem was that Rags couldn't go. Frank and I were distraught over losing our best friend, but there was simply no choice. So we were relieved when my grandparents agreed to let Rags come and stay with them on their farm in East Texas.

Although raised as a city dog, Rags quickly adapted to the routine of farm life and obviously enjoyed the freedom of the open spaces. She became a big help to my grandparents by learning to round up the dairy cows at the end of the day and bring them to the barn to be milked. Rags also became a real coon dog. One night she treed four raccoons in the same tree—"some kind of record," my granddad bragged.

Rags loved my grandmother and followed her around like a shadow. When Grandmother walked the quarter-mile to the mailbox, Rags went with her. When Grandmother went out to gather the eggs, Rags went with her but waited patiently outside the henhouse so she wouldn't scare the hens. When Grandmother went fishing at the pond west of the barn, Rags tagged along and slept on the bank of the pond or chased frogs until Grandmother was ready to go back to the house. They were constant companions. And Rags would have torn anyone or anything apart that made a harmful move toward my grandmother. In truth, she was even a little jealous of my granddad.

My grandparents' house was old-fashioned with a T-shaped porch that went completely across the front of the house on the south and through the middle of the house toward the north. There were five rooms in the house—two on the east and three on the west, each one with an outside wooden door and screen door that opened onto the middle porch. All this was under one big A-shaped roof.

As Grandmother worked from room to room, she often left the wooden doors open to enjoy the cool air, and Rags moved with her from one door to the other on the porch, watching her work, protecting her, and waiting for her to come outside to give her a scratch.

At age sixty-three, my grandmother died quietly in her bed from a heart attack. She died so quietly that my granddad, sleeping next to her, didn't know it until she didn't get up on time the next morning. Naturally the whole family grieved at her loss, but no one grieved more than Rags.

A few weeks later, my granddad came by my parents' home, and my mom asked him how he was doing.

"I'd be doing okay if it wasn't for Rags," he said. "She wanders up and down the porch, going from door to door, looking for Margie and whining. She's been doing it all day every day for weeks now. It's about to get the best of me."

"Well, Daddy, do you want us to come and get her?" (By this time we had moved back to the city.)

"No, she's the best dog I've ever had, and I need her. Besides, I know just how she feels about your mama."

My grandmother wasn't such an extraordinary woman, but any woman loved as she was loved by a dog like Rags must have been something special.

Dash, Dot, Dash

As a boy, the great inventor Thomas Edison learned Morse code and how to use a telegraph. After Edison's first wife died, he met Mina Miller, who became his sweetheart. Thomas taught Mina the Morse code, and after she had learned it, he decided to test her ability. So he tapped out a special message to her with a coin. When Mina successfully decoded the message, it was Thomas's proposal of marriage. She immediately tapped out her acceptance, and they were married.

Stopped by a Cop

$\mathscr{I}$ went to high school in a small town in central Texas. Now, when I say small, I mean small. The sign outside of town said, "Home of 923 nice people and one old grouch."

There were only twenty-one seniors in my graduating class, and our favorite pastime was to sit downtown on the corner and watch the through traffic stop and go at the only stoplight in town. They might not have to stay in our little town, but we at least made them stop and look both ways before they went on to bigger and better places.

My best friend's dad in that small town was a funeral director. My dad was the minister of a small church in town, and he worked for the funeral director part-time. Like many funeral homes of old, this one was in a big, old house. The family lived in one side, and the funeral home was operated out of the other side. Since there was no radio station in town, and the newspaper only came out once a week, the only way we knew someone was "lying in state" at the funeral home was if the front porch light was on. Then we had to call the funeral home and ask who it was, in case it was someone we knew. Since the funeral home was directly across the street from the post office, and there was no local mail delivery, everyone in town could see the front porch light every day when they went to get their mail. In short, it worked.

Several years after I graduated from high school, I was living in a large city about thirty miles from the small town. For a party I was having, and as a special joke for a friend's over-the-hill birthday, I borrowed an old, dilapidated child-size casket from my high-school friend's dad. I remembered it sitting in the storage area of the funeral home. We had used it a time or two to "bury our rivals" at pep rallies in high school.

It was a big hit at the party. The next evening, I put the little casket in the backseat of my car and drove down the freeway toward the small town to return it. About three miles outside of town, I was pulled over by a policeman, because I was speeding. When he came to the driver's window, I handed him my driver's license, a bit embarrassed by the incident.

"You're in a hurry, aren't you, ma'am?" he asked.

"Yes, I'm sorry, Officer."

"Where are you going in such a hurry?"

Without thinking, I motioned toward the backseat and replied, "To the funeral home in town."

The patrolman casually shined his flashlight into the backseat to see what I was transporting. Then he quickly did a double take and a startled look came over his face as he realized he was looking at a child's casket.

"Oh. I . . . I . . . I see," he stumbled. "Well . . . follow me!" And he turned and literally ran back through the darkness to his patrol car.

"Wait! Officer!" I called, suddenly realizing I had miscommunicated and wanting to tell him the truth. I even opened my door and started to go after him, but it was too late. He jumped into his car, flipped on his blinking lights and siren, and took off toward town, motioning for me to follow him. So, not knowing what else to do, I started my car and followed him into town.

When I arrived at the funeral home with a police escort, my friends at the funeral home were puzzled. Once again I tried to stop the policeman, but he just smiled sympathetically, waved, and drove away. And my friends became even more puzzled when I broke into gales of uncontrolled laughter.

Gettin' Thar

*H*iram had walked four long miles over the Great Smoky Mountains to court his lifelong sweetheart, Mary. They sat quietly for a long time on a bench beside Mary's log cabin. But soon that old devil moon worked its magic, and Hiram slid closer to Mary.

He patted her hand and said, "Mary, y'know I got a clearnin' over thar and a team an' a wagon an' some hawgs an' cows, an' I'low to build me a house this fall an' . . . ."

Mary's mother, who had just awakened, interrupted Hiram at this point. "Mary," she called in a loud voice, "is that young man thar yit?"

Mary responded with a giggle, "No, Maw, but he's gettin' thar."

Cappers Weekly

All for Love

🦅

When the war began, the young prince was called home from his foreign travels to help his father direct the war effort. Prince Jostin was torn between two loves—the love of his young wife, Elana, whom he had met and secretly married in one of his enemy's tiny country villages, and the love of his homeland and family.

At first refusing to answer the king's summons and leave his wife, Jostin became restless and depressed. He needed to be with Elana, but he also needed to be living up to his royal responsibilities. At the same time, Elana was frightened that her people would discover who Jostin really was and kill him or hold him hostage. Talking quietly long into the cold winter night, they finally agreed that Jostin must return home and leave Elana behind temporarily.

Just before dawn, after a long and teary good-bye, Jostin stole away into the darkness, accompanied by his two bodyguards, and escaped unnoticed over the border to his own country. Following the river northward, they finally arrived at the palace two days later.

For the next few months, Jostin immersed himself in his

royal duties as chief of the royal armies. He studied geo-graphical maps and laid careful strategies to help end the war quickly while avoiding the part of enemy territory where Elana and her family lived. At times his blood ran hot with fervor for his countrymen and against their neighbor-ing foes. At other times, his blood ran cold as he thought of what could happen to his beloved Elana if they discovered her marriage to him.

Jostin kept in touch with Elana through an underground messaging system of his fellow countrymen who had infil-trated the enemy lines and set up a secret relay line. Their messages of love and commitment traveled the under-ground along with coded military messages.

Late in the spring, Jostin received a message from Elana saying that she was five months pregnant. Jostin was elated! Then reality hit. Her pregnant condition would draw special attention to the fact that she had been with him. She would be in greater danger than ever now. Her note said that she was staying inside the house, but her family's friends and neighbors were beginning to question her parents about her change of behavior.

Then in early summer the underground message system was discovered by the enemy. A pouch of top-secret docu-ments and papers was confiscated, including a letter from Jostin to Elana. Realizing the great pawn Elana could be in the intensifying war game, an important general in the enemy army arrived unannounced at the home of Elana's parents early one morning and took her into custody. She was escorted in the general's private car to their military headquarters and locked in a bedroom there, with guards stationed at the door night and day.

When the news arrived at the palace by military attaché, Jostin was stricken with terror. His precious Elana . . . and their baby. What could he do? *I could gather our armies and cut straight down the river to their headquarters to rescue her. No, they would hear of our approach and kill her before I could ever get there. I could surrender. No, my father would never allow it. I could give myself in exchange for her. No, we would still not be together. God, help me know what to do!*

Calling for his official stationery, he wrote the following letter in his own handwriting to the enemy's queen:

> *I will do anything you say in order to secure the release of my wife, short of surrender or becoming a hostage. I love her more than anything in this life. Please tell me what you want, and I'll do it.*

A few days later, the queen's answer came in a heavily embossed envelope bearing the queen's personal seal. It said simply,

> *Prove your love for your wife, and I will let her come to you. Cut off your right hand and send it to us with your royal ring still on it.*

Without hesitation, the young prince called for a small

wooden chest to be brought to him. He wrote a short note to the queen and gave it to one of the guards. Then, telling his faithful bodyguards what to do, he pulled out his own sword and chopped off his right hand. Then he fainted.

The guards put the hand, with the royal ring on it, in the chest and took it directly to the queen. The guard handed her the note and chest. She opened the note and read,

If you had asked for both hands, I would have gladly complied.

When the queen opened the chest and saw the prince's severed hand, she was so moved by his great love for his wife and child, she released Elana and allowed her to return with the guards to Jostin. The guards also delivered to Jostin's father a letter from the queen requesting a truce.

Love, not hate, had ended the war.

The Secret of Staying in Love

✦

*A*t her golden wedding party, the older wife told guests the secret of her happy marriage.

"On my wedding day, I decided to make a list of ten of my husband's faults which, for the sake of our marriage, I would overlook."

As the guests were leaving, a young woman whose marriage had recently been in difficulties asked the older woman what some of the faults were that she had seen fit to overlook.

The older woman said, "To tell you the truth, my dear, I never did get around to listing them. But whenever my husband did something that made me hopping mad, I would say to myself, *Lucky for him that's one of the ten!*"

Paul Lee Tan

Encyclopedia of 7700 Illustrations

Give It Away!

On opening night of *South Pacific* on Broadway, musical star Mary Martin was handed a note as she was ready to go on stage. The note was handwritten from Oscar Hammerstein, who Mary knew was lying on his deathbed. The note said simply,

Dear Mary,

A bell's not a bell till you ring it. A song's not a song till you sing it. Love in your heart is not put there to stay. Love isn't love till you give it away.

Not Worth the Worry

$\mathcal{M}$y first paid writing job was on the personal staff of Dallas oil billionaire Haroldson Lafayette Hunt, better known as H. L. Hunt and recognized at the time as "the richest man in the world." My job was to write political comment columns that were syndicated nationally under the title "Hunt for Truth."

Naturally Mr. Hunt's being incredibly rich brought the press around on a regular basis. It was during one of those probing interviews, when reporters tried to make an aging-but-still-brilliant man into a bumbling fool, that Mr. Hunt, as usual, turned the tables on them. He sat at his desk with a piece of paper in his left hand, his wispy white hair mussed from running his right hand through it, waving the paper to emphasize his answers to their questions.

One reporter baited Mr. Hunt about his sporty son, Lamar, who had bought the Dallas Texas football team and moved them to Kansas where they became the Kansas City Chiefs. Predictably, during the transition years, his investment in the team was in the red.

The reporter said, "Mr. Hunt, Lamar has lost over a million

dollars a year on a football team. Doesn't that worry you?"

Mr. Hunt paused for a moment, as if mentally calculating, and then said, "Well, the way I figure it, if Lamar lost a million dollars a year, he'd be broke in about four hundred and fifty years." (Lamar was, of course, incredibly wealthy himself.) Then he grinned his "gotcha" grin, and his blue eyes twinkled with delight, as I'd seen them do so often. To him, it just wasn't worth the worry.

Like Lamar, you don't need to worry about a few minor losses along the way either, because your Father is incredibly rich. In fact, he owns the whole world.

———

Mary Hollingsworth

A Few Hallelujahs for Your Ho Hums

I've Been Thinking

$\mathcal{S}$ven and Hulda, a Scandinavian couple, were Christians. They sang in the choir; they were at Sunday school every Sunday; they had prayer at every meal; they went to all the church functions. But they could not get along.

At home it was terrible: bickering, complaining, fussing. After both of them had devotions one morning, separately, of course, Hulda said to Sven, "You know, Sven, I have been thinking. I got de answer to dis hopeless problem we're livin' wit. I tink ve should pray for de Lord to take vun of us home to be with Him. And then, Sven, I could go live wit my sister."

Bruce Larson
Believe and Belong

Moving On

🦅

When I was a kid, we moved around a lot. At last count, my mom and dad had moved forty-seven times. In fact, my mom once commented that we had moved so much that, when the television ever got accidentally unplugged, it wrapped its cord around itself and ran out on the front porch and waited to be loaded. She laughingly claimed that she could blow a whistle and our furniture would pile itself up in the corner.

Oh, go ahead and laugh, but there was one house in Greenville, Texas, that we moved in and out of three different times. And Greenville, not being a metropolis, only had two moving companies; so we had the same two men from Frank Wolfe Movers for all three moves.

The third time they came to move us out of the house on Caddo Street was like old home week. Those guys were practically part of the family by then. George asked about our dog, Rags, and Leroy wanted to know when we had bought the upright piano that wasn't there the last time they had moved us.

One thing was different during the third move though.

Harry, a new employee, also came from Wolfe to help with the move. You can imagine his surprise at the welcome home they received. Finally, tired of the unproductive conversation, he said, "George, we might as well start with this sofa."

(Pause: Now, this next statement was one of those you-know-you've-moved-too-often-when moments.)

George said, "No, Harry, you've got to go back there in the back bedroom and get that round oak table; it fits right up in the front corner of the truck."

Everybody laughed but Harry. Nonetheless, they loaded the round oak table first. And when we arrived at the new house, George and Leroy placed almost all the furniture in the right rooms with virtually no help from us.

Well, we should always be moving on, moving from the ho hums of life toward the hallelujahs, especially in our spiritual lives. If we do it often enough and get lots of practice, moving into our heavenly home will be the easiest move we ever make, especially if we use the same Moving Man every time.

Reading the Rule Book

$\mathcal{O}$n the floor of the United States Senate, the debate was prolonged and heated between two prominent senators. Each one fiercely defended and promoted his personal stance on the issue at hand. As the discussion progressed, though, the debate became personal for the two. Finally, one of the men stood up, pointed his finger at the other senator, and yelled, "Oh, why don't you just go to hell!"

The second senator, taken aback and greatly offended by his colleague's demand, turned to the podium in outrage and pleaded with President Calvin Coolidge: "Mr. President, did you hear that?"

Looking up from the document he had been studying and over the top of his reading glasses at the offended senator, President Coolidge said with a serious look, "You know, sir, I have been reading the Rule Book, and it says you don't have to go."

To Lament or Laugh

> It better befits a man to laugh at life
> than to lament over it.
>
> Seneca

*W*hen my friend Charlotte moved into her new house, we spent several hours unpacking boxes and finally worked our way into the kitchen. She wanted to wash all the dishes before putting them away, so we unpacked a couple of boxes and loaded the dishes into the new dishwasher, only to discover that we couldn't find the automatic dishwashing detergent.

I said, "That's no problem; we'll just use this dishwashing liquid."

"Are you sure?" she asked. "I thought you couldn't use regular liquid detergent in a dishwasher."

"Oh, not really," I assured her. "I've done it before, and it worked fine."

"Okay, if you say so." (Friendship can be so misguided at times.)

So I filled up both detergent cups on the dishwasher door, closed the door, and turned on the dishwasher. Then we went back into the dining room to continue unpacking that part of the house.

About twenty minutes later, I decided it was time to call it a night. So I picked up my coat and started for the front door. On the way, I had to pass the kitchen, and I casually glanced in. The entire kitchen floor was covered with soapsuds! And they were getting deeper by the second. But I didn't panic.

I calmly turned to Charlotte and said, "You know, Char, you were right. You can't use liquid detergent in a dishwasher after all." *She* panicked!

The next hour was like a rerun of an *I Love Lucy* show. Every time I pushed the sponge mop into the soapsuds, the whole sudsy floor moved away from me like a glacier. Charlotte finally held a widemouthed pan to the floor, and I chased the suds into the pan with the mop. She would then pour them into the sink, rinse them down with cold water, and we'd start again.

We were winning the battle until we ventured to open the dishwasher door to face a solid wall of soapsuds. We quickly slammed the door shut, trapping most of the suds inside. We decided the thing to do was to put the dishwasher on "rinse" to wash away the suds.

Wrong! The hot water just multiplied the soapsuds and sent them bubbling onto the kitchen floor again. And we were back to square one. At that point, we couldn't decide whether to laugh or cry. So we just laughed and mopped.

Finally, using the sprayer hose on the sink, we were able to dissolve the suds in the dishwasher with cold water. By then we were so tired from mopping and laughing we just went to bed. We decided that it was not the ideal method to employ but that she did, in fact, have the cleanest kitchen floor we'd ever seen.

Everything I Need to Know as a Woman I Learned from Lucille Ball

$\mathcal{I}$ grew up watching the old black-and-white "I Love Lucy" show on television, laughing myself silly all the while. As I became a woman, I was able to apply some of the lessons that I learned from Lucille Ball to daily life. Here are some things I learned:

Life is never really black and white. *You* have to add the color. ✴ Never, never, never tell your age. ✴ Always keep your roots covered. ✴ Reading directions is for wimps. ✴ Never marry a foreigner. ✴ If you can't speak the language, shout. ✴ Never admit to anything. ✴ Spaghetti isn't done if it won't stick to the ceiling. ✴ Anytime you mess up, cry. ✴ Anytime they're chasing you, cry. ✴ Anytime you get caught, cry. ✴ Don't worry; whatever it is, you can hide it in the closet. ✴ To make something fit, diet, dye it, or dry it. ✴ Beware of wax fruit, wax tulips, and wax noses. ✴ Sticking to your budget shows no creativity. ✴ Getting a job is easy; it's keeping it that's hard. ◄ Grape juice won't wash off your feet. ◄ Always keep a good scheme brewing. ◄ Have a good disguise with you at all times. ◄ When you meet important people, do something stupid to get their attention. ◄ If you want to be a big success, sing off key. ◄ Never tango with eggs in your pocket. ◄ And when all else fails, laugh, Honey, laugh.

The True Secret of Happiness

Natasha Josefowitz

Every day have

something to do

or somewhere to go.

Every day have

someone to call,

someone to see,

someone to love.

But most important,

every day have

something to give

to someone.

A Logical Question

$\mathcal{M}$y niece Kim was only three years old. Her sisters, Ronda and Julie, were about five and seven. They lived with their parents, Loren and Penny, and grandparents, my in-laws, better known as Mom and Dad, on a Kansas wheat farm where they also raised cattle.

One Sunday morning, Dad noticed that one of the cows was about ready to birth her calf, and from past experience, he thought she might need some help. So he closed her in a stall in the barn. Then the family went to church.

After church, they all hurried home to see how the cow was doing. Sure enough, she was in hard labor in the barn. So Dad and Loren quickly changed clothes and started out the door to the barn.

"Can we go, Daddy?" asked Ronda.

Looking at Penny, he said, "What do you think?"

"They have to learn sometime," she said. "It might as well be now as later, I guess."

"Okay, let's go then," said Loren, "but you have to stay out of the way so the old cow doesn't kick you."

The birthing process was a long, arduous ordeal, as Dad

had suspected it would be. After forty-five minutes of huffing, puffing, and using pulling chains, they finally smiled as the little white-faced, spindly-legged calf was born. Dad and Loren, not to mention the cow, were exhausted.

The two men leaned against the barn wall to catch their breath, wipe the sweat off their faces, and admire the wobbly calf. It was at that precise moment that little Kim, peering between the rails of the stall, chose to pose a three-year-old's logical question.

"Well, Daddy," she said seriously, "just how'd that thing get in there anyway?"

Now if you think Loren was out of breath before, that innocent question really caused him to suck air. But, it was, after all, a logical question from a three-year-old viewpoint, don't you think?

The Atonement

$\mathcal{P}$ersonal appearance was not something that was of great concern to author Samuel Clemens (Mark Twain). One day he and his wife went to visit some friends and, as usual, Mark did not choose to wear the expected necktie. Instead, he wore his shirt open at the neck for comfort. His wife, embarrassed again by his unsightly appearance, read him the riot act when they returned home.

To atone for his breach of manners, Twain went to his closet and chose the best tie he had that would have matched the outfit he had worn that day. He wrapped it in a box, wrote a note to go with it, and then mailed the package to the friends they had visited.

The note said that, since he had neglected to wear the tie, they might like to look at it for half an hour and then return it.

Last Day on Earth

※

$\mathcal{D}$r. Carlyle knew, a moment after he inserted the needle and watched the fluid drain slowly into his arm, that something had gone wrong.

It came to him, in a slow crystallization of horror, that the test tubes were not in their right order. And when he checked the numbers again, with an almost desperate precision, he saw what he had done.

He, Dr. William Roy Carlyle, at the peak of a great career in research, had injected himself with almost certain death.

He stared at the needle on the table, and while he watched, a strange light crept over it. Dawn! He raised his eyes and saw the day come through the high windows of his laboratory—gentle and golden, like a woman with her arms outstretched. His *last* dawn?

He pushed himself up from the table and crossed the room on stiff, trembling legs. The sky was flushed with a spreading light, and the east sides of all the great buildings of the city had turned gold in the rising sun. He stared at it, like an exile about to be banished from a loved country. And he knew in that bitter moment that though forty-three years of his life were spent, he had never really seen the dawn before.

Too often it had merely meant a time to stop work, after some laboratory experiment carried on far into the night; a symbol that he must admit another grueling failure to find his way through the pathless forest of science.

But now, in this quickened instant, he saw the dawn for what it was: bright, gilded, promising, offering its twelve daylight hours without favor or prejudice to all on earth to do with as they pleased.

He turned away from it, passing a hand across his eyes and down over the short stubble of beard that grew along his jaw. His arm had begun to swell slowly, almost imperceptibly, in the area of the injection.

This was the way it worked—763X—slow as a drowsing rattlesnake, just as deadly when it struck. The white mice they'd tested had appeared normal for six hours after the injections. Then, just when it seemed the experiment would succeed, death had struck through both cages—violent and irrevocable.

Carlyle thrust the memory from his mind. He had tried this experiment on himself against the advice of his coworkers and his own better judgment—tried it in a moment of exhaustion, when fatigue stood at his elbow, fogging his vision, clouding his mind.

Reaching for 764X, he had accidentally taken up the old 763X, the very serum that had already been tested and proved fatal!

Now, too late, he saw what his error would cost him. There was no known antidote. He must see this day through with the cool detachment science had ingrained in him. For it would be his last experiment. His last day on earth.

He took up his pencil and began to jot the necessary data in his notebook in a quick, jerky scrawl. There was a slim chance that he could still be of some use. Science might learn through his error.

Semler came in before he'd quite finished, and with a brief nod, set about his work. It gave Carlyle a strange feeling—like a spy almost—to watch young Semler, so sure of life, frowning over his test tubes. He wanted to warn the younger man, to tell him that life was only a loan, and a brief loan at that—and that he must spend it well, spend it now!

"Semler—" he began. But the fierce discipline that the laboratory forced upon them made the words come hard. He rose restlessly and crossed the room to the window.

Spring had laid her first magic across the city in a pale web of green. Between the bricks and masonry, in empty lots and neglected backyards, the earth had come alive again, resurgent and triumphant.

"How long," Carlyle wondered aloud, "how long, Semler, since you've taken a real vacation and gotten into the country, where there's fresh earth and open sky overhead and plenty of air to fill your lungs?"

Semler was staring at him strangely through his heavy-lensed glasses. There was something about the young scientist both confused and childlike, as if he had become lost in the world of test tubes and could not find his way out again.

How gaunt he was, Carlyle thought! No color in his lean face; even his blue eyes, strained and weak from research, seemed to have faded to a paler blue than they'd been when he first came here.

"Vacation?" Semler said. "Why, not in a good while, sir. My wife went away . . ." he dreamed over it for a moment. "She went to Cape Cod for two weeks last summer. She told me about it—the surf and the sand dunes. I meant to get up for a weekend"—he glanced down at the glass slide in the palm of his gloved hand—"but you know how it is."

Yes, Carlyle knew. But a feeling of guilt, so poignant that it seemed almost too much to bear, seemed to take his heart and twist it. For he had never known until today that Semler had a wife. He didn't know where the man lived, where he had been born, who his parents were, what fears or doubts or dreams lived with him in his private world. He had never, in the three years they'd worked together, even asked after Semler's health.

If Semler was ill, it meant lost time on an experiment. But oh, how much he had looked past in this young assistant of his! How vulnerable Semler was—how lost and life-hungry!

"I'm arranging for you to leave for a month's vacation," Carlyle said now. "You must put your work aside and take time off. You'll come back with a fresh viewpoint, Semler. You'll see."

Semler set the slide down. His fingers in the rubber gloves trembled a bit. "But we're so close to the serum we're looking for," he protested. "Another week, another month, and we'll have it! Sir, 764X may even be the one."

Carlyle's arm had begun to throb a little, and the swelling, though still scarcely perceptible, had fanned out now in a slightly larger area. He smiled at Semler—a strange dry smile.

"Haven't we always been close to the answer, Semler? Hasn't it always been another week? Another month? Another year? Meanwhile life slipped by and all the things we promised ourselves slipped by with it. Don't wait! Take your vacation while you're young and there's still time." He turned his back to conceal the emotion he knew must show in his face.

When he'd regained control of his voice again, he said evenly, "I've some business to attend. I'm taking the day off. Tomorrow"—he chose his words carefully—"tomorrow I may be called away. All my latest findings are there, Semler, if you need to refer to them. On the last page of my notebook."

He held out his hand briefly and shook Semler's gloved one. *Carry on!* his soul whispered. Then he turned and hurried down the dark, soundless corridor.

Outside the spring sun shone warmly on his back, and as he made his way along the crowded street, the very air seemed to seduce him.

Had spring ever been so gentle, so endearing before? Had every little scene, every shop window, every face he passed ever been so wonderfully interesting? Yes, there was a time . . . he struggled to remember. And he knew suddenly when it had been—the year he'd fallen in love. That gave him the answer. Now that he must leave it, he had fallen in love with life.

At Sixty-Second Street, he hailed a cab and gave the driver his home address. It would take a little explaining, coming home this way when he'd planned just to take a short nap in the laboratory and work the rest of the day. But he'd figure it out some way. Spring fever, he'd call it. He smiled. Life fever—that's what it came closer to being.

He stared out the cab window all the way home, pressed forward in the seat, so that when the cab stopped suddenly, he was jolted against the door. Had the forsythia bloomed this morning? Why hadn't he seen it? And the grass along the drive—it couldn't have gotten green in a single day!

Almost, it seemed, fate was mocking him. And yet he knew that was not true. His blind past was mocking this brief stretch of present.

When she heard his ring at the door, his wife came running. "Roy," she called out, "Roy, is anything wrong?"

He stood on the threshold and watched her open the door to him. Mary, his wife. Just so, she had opened her life to him ten years ago. Mary, with her soft hair, like a wreath of golden sunlight, and her blue eyes that still could look at him as if he contained her world.

He caught her against him, soundlessly, wordlessly, and rocked her for a moment.

She struggled in his arms. "Roy, Roy," she cried, "something's gone wrong—terribly wrong! My darling, what is it?"

He felt the trembling deep inside him, the terrible trembling. For of all the bonds that held him to life, this was the strongest, the deepest.

How could he kiss her, knowing that it would be the last time?

"Nothing's wrong," he managed. "Only that it's spring, and I decided to take a day off. I promised Felice I'd take her to the park. Where's Felice?"

At the mention of her name, his little girl bounded in from the back room.

"Daddy!" she cried and flung herself upon him. "Oh, Daddy-daddy-daddy!"

Was that how it had always sounded, the funny little music of her voice, the sound of his name when she said it? Had her hair always been this way to his touch, silken and smelling of soap?

He caught her under her arms and swung her high in the air so that her starched dress fanned out behind her. "How's my big girl?" he asked, searching her dancing gray eyes. She hung around his neck, kicking and laughing, overjoyed at this surprise visit at the start of a routine day.

"We're going to the park," he announced. "Remember, Felice, I promised I'd take you—oh, a long time ago?"

Three *years* ago? Yes, three long springs ago, when Semler had first come to him to work on 124X, and they'd thought they would have the answer with 125X.

"We'll buy you a balloon," he'd promised Felice, "any color you want, and we'll have lunch outside, under the big umbrellas. How will you like that?"

She'd almost burst with joy and sung that wonderful song—that wonderful, wonderful song that went, "Oh, Daddy-daddy-daddy!"

And he'd let three years slip by with 124X, 125X—like stones around his neck weighing down his whole life. Why hadn't he stolen a day, or even an hour of all that time? He never would have missed it!

"Hurry now," he told Felice. "Put on your hat and button your pink coat. We're all three going. You and Mother and I."

Hurry now, hurry now. Only a few more hours were left to him.

Hurry downstairs, hurry into the cab. Hurry down bright Fifth Avenue, where the sun glints on taxicab roofs, and the nursemaids push little pink-blanketed bundles with rattles swinging above them and a whole life to spend. Hurry now, hurry now. But see everything. Love everything. Taste and enjoy and exult in everything.

Oh, this is the way he should always have felt, through all the drab, weighted days when he had worried over the rent, his work, a rude word from a cabby—when he had wasted time, time, which was life's elixir.

He took Mary's hand in his. He must remember, like a lesson he'd learned, not to press her hand too hard. Not to say anything that would let her know. She would know soon, much too soon, anyway.

They took one of the rowboats and sailed across the lagoon, Roy in the center rowing, Felice in the back, and Mary in the front. It was so calm that all the buildings of Manhattan looked down and preened themselves in the water, and the proud white swans seemed to slip by on glass.

Felice had a lollipop, and she hung off the back of the rowboat, trailing her hand in the water, laughing and showing her starched white petticoat. Oh, it was a beautiful ride!

But the sun was climbing, climbing. And his arm had swollen so that very often now, he had to rest the oars and his arms.

Mary moved back in the boat and put her head on his shoulder. He did not tell her that his shoulder had begun to ache, or that he felt tired.

And he did not tell Felice that the merry-go-round was a terrible effort, and when he climbed up on the child-sized black horse, he felt he had climbed a mountain.

And when 3:00 drew near, and he knew that he must go home, must make them take him home—he tried to sit straight in the cab. He tried to forget about the white mice and how they had died in their cages, and to concentrate, instead, on this day—this golden day of spring that had been the best of his whole life.

He thought he was doing well at it, even in the elevator. And then, just as Mary put her key in the lock, he heard her scream his name, and he felt his head strike the door . . .

The lost thread of time came back to him slowly, and with it came consciousness, heavy and smothering. Something was reaching for him—black, formless, awful. He sank again. Then he saw the white blur of a room and heard someone's name being called. It was a moment before he knew it was his own name—Mary's voice calling him.

When he forced open his eyes, he saw Semler bending over him, breathing heavily, his eyes pale behind his thick-lensed glasses. "You're going to be all right, sir," Semler said. "They told us so this morning."

This morning? What morning? And suddenly, startlingly, while Carlyle struggled to remember, Semler fell on his knees beside the bed. "Dr. Carlyle, 763X—it's fatal to the test animals, but it can be used on human beings. Do you know what that means, sir? It means we're on the brink . . . on the very brink of our great discovery!"

Carlyle endeavored to piece the words together, slowly, with a great effort. 763X! Like a key in a lock, it swung back the door of memory. The terrible moment after the injection when he realized what he'd done . . . the dawn and the way the sky had looked . . . Semler, that new Semler he had never quite known before . . . the street . . . the sweet smell of spring and life . . . Mary . . . Felice . . . the lagoon . . . and now . . . perhaps the great discovery!

He smiled a wan smile and motioned Semler closer. "Tell them . . ." he began, and then he shook his head and fell silent. For the world would not be interested in his greatest discovery. The one he'd made yesterday—that every day should be lived as if it were the last day—the last day on earth.

———

Frances Ancker and Cynthia Hope

You Not American!

$\mathcal{M}$y wife and I were traveling in Eastern Europe with Bob and Marjean Ingram. When we crossed the border from Hungary to Romania three burly, rough-looking soldiers boarded the train to check our passports and examine our luggage.

Their leader indicated that he wanted to see our passports. As we handed them to him he pointed to our luggage. As I rose to reach for a large suitcase, he suddenly stopped me. In broken English he said, "Wait! You not American!"

Then he looked at Marjean and said, "You not American."

I must confess that I was gripped by a vise of fear. The man pointed to a paper bag Marjean had on the seat beside her. "What is that?" he asked, pointing to the edges of a book that protruded out of the top of the bag.

Marjean pulled out her Bible. I gulped, thinking to myself, *Now we are in real trouble.*

The policeman took the Bible and began to leaf through its pages. He opened to the Book of Ephesians and pointed to 2:19. He ordered: "Read."

We read it aloud: "Now, therefore, you are no longer

strangers and foreigners, but fellow citizens with the saints and members of the household of God."

Instantly the policeman's face radiated with a benevolent smile as he said, "You not American. I not Romanian. We are citizens of heaven."

Then he turned to his fellow officers and said, "These people okay." He returned our passports and bid us Godspeed.

Thank God for your citizenship in heaven!

———

R. C. Sproul

In the Presence of God

The Great Boating Excursion

*A*fter we had been married about ten years, my husband decided we would get a boat and take up skiing and fishing. Sounded like a good idea at the time.

The first time we went out was to Lake Grapevine for a trial run. About a half-hour before dark, we headed back to the marina, and he asked me, "Do you want to get the truck and trailer down the ramp, or do you want to drive the boat up on the trailer?" I said I didn't know how to back up a trailer, and I'd rather drive the boat up.

He went after the truck while I idled the boat in the harbor. When he got the trailer positioned on the ramp, I steered the boat into position, lined it up squarely, gave it the gas, and headed for the V at the front of the trailer. Mind you, the only boat driving I had done was to pull a skier, and that's how I took off for that trailer. R-r-r-r-rmp! I went airborne right through that V and into the bed of the truck.

Now, a marina is always very noisy—lots of people yelling, laughing, revving engines, kids screaming, even dogs barking. But when I drove the boat into the truck, an immediate hush fell on the place. It reminded me of that old commercial that said, "When E. F. Hutton speaks . . ." *dead* silence.

We repaired the boat and the truck and made another run at fun on the lake. We went to Lake Texoma next. When it was time to leave, my husband said, "This time, *I'll* drive the boat. You bring the truck around. It's a four-lane ramp, and nobody is there. Just back straight down the ramp."

So I took the truck and started to back down this four-lane ramp. I would go back five feet, and the trailer would go to the left. I'd pull up, back down five feet, and the trailer would go to the right. For forty-five minutes I went up, back, right, up, back, left, while my husband stood in the boat groaning and turning red—not from the sun either.

Finally, some man came walking by. He asked if I needed help. I got out of the truck and said, "Please back this truck down that ramp." He did.

We made the three-hour drive from Lake Texoma to home in silence . . . *heavy* silence. But we didn't give up. When we got home, the navigator told me that I would learn how to back a trailer . . . or else. The next day I was to practice in our driveway until I could do it. We had a circular driveway. I practiced entering from the left, and I practiced entering from the right. I practiced going down the straight of the driveway and around the circle. And I conquered. I did learn how to back that trailer, and I was proud. *I'm ready now,* I thought.

So off we went to Lake Livingston for another fun adventure. It came time to leave. No sweat. I knew what to do. I'd practiced this. This ramp was only one lane. No problem. It was as wide as our driveway. I backed the truck and trailer down that ramp straight as an arrow. I grinned, feeling like a Cheshire cat, content and satisfied, until I heard him yelling, "Stop! STOP! STOP! Oh, no! Why didn't you stop?"

Well, nobody had told me when to stop, and I was trying to get as close to the boat as I could. Now, I haven't tested all boat ramps, but that boat ramp had a big-drop off at the end of the concrete. (It was under water; so who knew?) I had backed so far that the trailer dropped off, still attached to the trailer hitch, but now hanging down in the water at a right angle to the truck.

Pulling the truck forward wouldn't lift the trailer. That just made it bang against the ramp. And six men couldn't lift it up against the water. So we had to call a maritime wrecker with a special winch that goes out into the water. After only a couple of hours we were out and on our way home . . . in silence, *dead* silence.

As we approached home, I timidly asked, "Do we want to continue having this much fun?" I really felt as if I'd had all the fun I could take. And I haven't been in a boat since.

———

Anita Brock
Divorce Recovery

Placed by Providence

(From a letter to her husband as the Constitution of the United States was being drawn up.)

I desire you would remember the ladies and be more generous and favorable to them than your ancestors. Do not put such unlimited power into the hands of the husbands. Remember, all men would be tyrants if they could. If particular care and attention is not paid to the ladies, we are determined to foment a rebellion, and will not hold ourselves bound by any laws in which we have no voice or representation. . . . Men of sense in all ages abhor those customs which treat us only as the vassals of your sex; regard us then as being placed by Providence under your protection, and in imitation of the Supreme Being make use of that power only for our happiness.

Abigail Adams

Let's Move On

Recently I shared a meal with some friends. A husband and wife wanted to tell me about a storm they were weathering. Through a series of events, she learned of an act of infidelity that had occurred over a decade ago. He had made the mistake of thinking it'd be better not to tell her, so he didn't. But she found out. And, as you can imagine, she was deeply hurt.

Through the advice of a counselor, the couple dropped everything and went away for several days. A decision had to be made. Would they flee, fight, or forgive?

So they prayed. They talked. They walked. They reflected. In this case the wife was clearly in the right. She could have left. Women have done so for lesser reasons. Or she could have stayed and made his life a living hell.

On the tenth night of their trip, my friend found a card on his pillow. On the card was a printed verse: "I'd rather do nothing with you than something without you." Beneath the verse she had written these words:

I forgive you. I love you. Let's move on.

The card might as well have been a basin. And the pen might as well have been a pitcher of water, for out of it poured pure mercy, and with it she washed her husband's feet. Certain conflicts can be resolved only with a basin of water.

———

Max Lucado
Just Like Jesus

My Wish for You

✵

I wish you some new love of lovely things, and some new forgetfulness of the teasing things, and some higher pride in the praising things, and some sweeter peace from the hurrying things, and some closer fence from the worrying things.

———

John Ruskin

Flocks or Socks?

One of our family's favorite stories is about Larry, our lighthearted son, who was always looking for a little mischief. One year, when he was scheduled to appear in our church's Christmas program to sing "As Shepherds Watched Their Flocks by Night," he jokingly practiced for weeks at home, singing, "As shepherds washed their socks at night."

The whole family was in stitches every time he broke into that chorus; in fact, at one point, I offered him five dollars if he would get up in front of the church and, like Frank Sinatra, do it "his way." (I guess I've always been one who's perpetually looking for a little mischief too!)

Well, he acted horrified that I even suggested it and accused me of bribing him to "commit a crime." On the night of the Christmas program, his stomach was full of butterflies, and his little heart was racing because he was so nervous. He shakily stepped up to his spot on the platform, took a big breath, and—you guessed it—unintentionally burst out with, "As shepherds washed their socks at night!"

That was the most memorable Christmas program for our family. But we weren't alone in having some unintentional holiday gaffes. I'm reminded of the time the art class was setting up a Christmas scene on the school lawn, and one of the boys asked uncertainly, "Where do we put the three wise guys?"

Then there were the four youngsters in the Christmas pageant each carrying a letter to form the word "S-T-A-R," but they went up in reverse order, accidentally spelling "R-A-T-S." I love that!

———

Barbara Johnson
Living Somewhere Between Estrogen and Death

The Anniversary

One Friday morning in the spring of 1970, a young hippie couple from the big city showed up on the doorstep of a little country church. Sid and Lani had been living together for two years, and Lani was six months pregnant.

"We want to get married as soon as possible," they told the minister in his study.

The minister was rather indignant at this interruption by bedraggled flower children who regarded his nice church as little more than a roadside wedding chapel. Hoping that a delay would discourage them, he said, "If you will attend church on Sunday, I will marry you after the morning service." The minister was confident that he would never see them again.

But on Sunday morning, the minister looked out to see the couple in the congregation, quite the sight in their long hair and ragged bell-bottoms. When the sanctuary was nearly empty, Sid and Lani met the minister at the altar for a simple ceremony. When congregation members realized that a wedding was about to take place, about thirty people hurried back into the church, happy to participate in the festivities of the strangers.

"Why are they here?" Lani asked, bewildered.

The minister said, "I guess they just care about you."

After the brief ceremony, Mildred, one of the women in the congregation, stood and asked the couple, "Where are you two going for your honeymoon?" Mildred and Jack had celebrated their twenty-fifth wedding anniversary only days earlier.

"I don't know," Sid said with a shrug. "Maybe up into the mountains to camp."

"Well, first you need dinner and a wedding cake," she announced with a warm smile. "You are coming to our house for dinner. In fact, everyone is invited to our house for dinner."

While the minister busied the couple signing certificates, Mildred hastily organized a potluck. When the couple and the minister arrived at Mildred's home twenty minutes later, the table was spread with sandwiches and salads. In the center of the table was the top layer of Mildred and Jack's anniversary cake.

The celebration went on for six hours. Lunch and cake were consumed, and the bride and groom were cheered and congratulated. They left that evening beaming at the heartfelt hospitality of the small congregation.

Two and one-half decades later, a middle-aged couple

drove up to the same little country church. They explained to the current minister that they had been married in the sanctuary twenty-five years earlier and engulfed by the loving congregation on their wedding day.

The minister had never heard the story, but a woman working in the office overheard the conversation. "I remember you," she said to the couple. "I was here that day and attended your wedding. Mildred is still in town. You must come to lunch with us."

Sitting at the table with the two elderly women, Sid and Lani told their story. The first eleven years of their marriage had been disastrous. Sid was on drugs, and Lani was an alcoholic. One day, with their lives on the verge of collapse, Sid said, "We have been to church only once in our lives—the day we were married. It was a good experience for us. Maybe we should go again." They attended a church near their home, gave their lives to Christ, and were transformed.

"It's our twenty-fifth anniversary," Sid told the women, "and we just had to return to the little church that means so much to us."

Today Sid and Lani are Christian drug counselors in the city. They freely admit that it was the love and acceptance of a congregation of farm folk for a couple of dirty hippies that ultimately turned their lives around and saved their marriage.

All around us there are people like Sid and Lani in need

of genuine, transforming love. Each of us has the opportunity to be a Mildred to such people every day.

———

Josh McDowell and Norm Geisler
Love Is Always Right

Still Smiling

$\mathcal{D}$r. Richard Selzer once removed a tumor from a young woman's face, requiring the severing of a facial nerve and leaving one side of her mouth lifeless and crooked. The surgeon was concerned about how the woman and her husband would respond to her new appearance. He relates what happened this way:

Her husband is in the room. He stands on the opposite side of the bed, and together, they seem to dwell in the evening lamplight. Isolated from me, private.

Who are they, I ask myself, he and this wry-mouth I have made, who gaze at each other, and touch each other generously, greedily?

The young woman speaks: "Will I always be like this?" she asks.

"Yes," I say. "It's because the nerve was cut."

She nods and is silent. But the young man smiles. "I like it," he says. "It's kind of cute."

He bends to kiss her crooked mouth, and I am so close I can see how he twists his own lips to accommodate hers, to show that their kiss still works. I remember that the angels sometimes appeared in Bible times as mortals, and I hold my breath and wonder.

———

Dr. Richard Selzer

Mortal Lessons: Notes on the Art of Surgery, adapted

The Chair by the Bedside

*O*nce there was an old man who longed for a deeper life of prayer. After trying unsuccessfully to comprehend scholarly books on the subject, he finally tried praying in a very childlike manner—by picturing Jesus seated in the chair beside his bed and talking to him. He found that he liked it so much, he did it "a couple of hours every day."

When the old man fell ill, he confessed to the local priest this habit of daily "having a conversation with Jesus."

"I'm careful, though," he told the priest. "If my daughter saw me talking to an empty chair, she'd . . . send me off to the funny farm."

The priest, profoundly moved by the old man's story, promised not to reveal his secret.

Two days later the old man's daughter called the priest to tell him of her father's death.

"Did he seem to die in peace?" the priest asked. The daughter assured him that her father had indeed gone quite peacefully.

"But there was something strange," she said reflectively. "In fact, beyond strange, kind of weird. Apparently just before Daddy died, he leaned over and rested his head on the chair beside his bed."

———

Brennan Manning

Abba's Child: The Cry of the Heart for Intimate Belonging

The Singer

$\mathcal{M}$ichael, my boy, you might as well forget about being a singer. You'll never be able to sing. You just can't do it."

The little dark-haired Italian boy stared in disbelief at his junior-high-school music teacher. Not sing? But singing was the only thing he really cared about in life. His dad was a wonderful singer. And he wanted to be a singer too. He had planned to be a great Italian tenor. And his favorite dream was to stand on the hills overlooking Rome, Italy, their family's homeland, and sing *"O Sole Mio"* with joy and reverence.

Michael ducked his head to hide the tears that leaped into his dark eyes, mumbled something, and walked out of the music room for the last time. The next day he had his class schedule changed to drop music. And he gave up singing forever. The unthinking teacher spoke daunting words that snuffed out the candle of his young dream.

For fifty-three years Michael pursued other things. He built a successful career in international business, becoming a consultant who was highly sought after by corporations around the world. He married Betty and cared for his family joyfully and well. And his life was surrounded by friends and associates who loved him. Still, his dream to sing simmered in a recess of his mind, like a slow-cooking soup on a back burner.

On New Year's Eve 1986, Michael and Betty went to a party at a friend's house. My friend Charlotte Greeson was at the same party. During the course of the evening, Michael met Charlotte, who's a marvelously talented music teacher, vocal coach, and conductor—a warm and sensitive lady.

"I've always wanted to sing," said Michael, "but I can't."

"How do you know you can't?" Charlotte asked him.

"Well, I've known it since I was a kid. My junior-high music teacher told me so."

"I bet you can sing *now*," said Charlotte smiling confidently. "No boy can sing well when his voice is changing in junior high."

"No, I'm sure I can't. Besides, it's too late—I'm sixty-six years old. But thanks for saying so."

"Michael, in the twenty-five years I've been teaching voice, I've never met anyone of any age that I couldn't teach to sing. I doubt seriously that you're the exception."

The flame of Michael's old dream flickered weakly. "Are you serious?" asked Michael. "Do you really think I could learn to sing at my age?"

"Well, of course you can. You're obviously extremely bright, and besides, I'm a good teacher. Together we'll do well. Anyway, what have you got to lose by trying?"

"When can we start?" asked Michael eagerly.

"Call me Monday," she said, giving him her card, "and we'll set up a lesson schedule."

When Michael came for his first voice lesson the next week, he couldn't even match pitch with the piano. For fifty-three years he had done exactly what his junior-high-school teacher had told him to do—he'd forgotten about singing. His unused singing voice had to start from scratch, literally.

Before long, though, Michael began to improve. And over the next three years of voice lessons, he showed good ability and amazing determination to sing. He worked hard, and gradually he became an able, if not virtuoso, Italian tenor at age sixty-nine.

On a gentle Texas spring night in 1990, several friends were at Charlotte's home watching television. The doorbell rang, and Charlotte went to answer it. Western Union was there to deliver a telegram, which read:

CHARLOTTE, JUST SANG "O SOLE MÍO" FROM HILLS ABOVE ROME. STOP. MY DREAM HAS COME TRUE. STOP. THANKS FOR YOUR ENCOURAGEMENT. DON'T STOP. LOVE, MICHAEL.

M. Norvel Young
Living Lights, Shining Stars

The Warp and Woof

The warp and woof of life is woven one day at a time. One day adds a strand of brightness and light. The next day adds a dark strand of shadows and depth. It is all the colors and hues carefully woven together that create the masterpiece God envisioned in the beginning. He sits at the eternal spinning wheel slowly turning it, feeding in the light and dark threads at precisely the right places to fashion a life worth living. And he smiles when the picture of you is complete—beautiful, interesting, and unique.

No More Room

*O*n a cold winter day in Philadelphia, Pennsylvania, a little girl named Hatti Wiatt, in a ragged coat and paper-thin shoes, came to a small church and asked to attend their Sunday school. It was explained to Hatti that, unfortunately, because their building was so small, there was just no room for her. So Hatti turned and sadly walked back through the snow to her tiny room where she lived alone.

Two years later, little Hatti became ill and died. Under her pillow was found a torn pocketbook with fifty-seven pennies in it. The pennies were wrapped carefully in a scrap of paper on which Hatti had written these words:

To help build the little church bigger,
so that more children can go to Sunday school.

For two years Hatti had painstakingly saved her pennies for the cause that was nearest her heart.

When the minister of the little church was handed the ragged pocketbook and its fifty-seven pennies, he wept. Then he told Hatti's story to the little church. The people were so moved that they began making donations to make little Hatti's dream come true. Newspapers told the story far and wide, too, and within five years those fifty-seven pennies had grown to $250,000—enough money in those days to build a large church building.

Today in Philadelphia stands a great church building that seats 3,300 people, a college with accommodations for more than 1,400 students, a Christian hospital, and a Sunday school facility so large that all who wish to learn may come.

It's amazing what one little girl, a dream, and fifty-seven pennies used for good can accomplish.

Paul Lee Tan

Encyclopedia of 7700 Illustrations

For Love and Roses

Comedian Jack Benny, while being one of the funniest actors in our recent history, also had a tender, loving side. He was completely in love with his wife, who stayed by his side for decades, through tough times and terrific times.

When Jack finally "arrived" as a recognized and sought-after comedian, and his financial status soared accordingly, he began sending his lovely wife a single, long-stemmed, red rose every day to thank her for her loyalty and to express his undying love.

This practice went on for many years. Every single day of every week of every year, the beautiful rose arrived faithfully at the door of their home. Even when Jack was out of town or overseas, the roses kept coming, reminding her of his never-failing love and devotion.

When Jack eventually died, his lifelong partner grieved bitterly, as would be expected. Unexpectedly, however, the single red rose continued to be delivered to her every day for over a week after the funeral. Finally, although it seemed so unlikely, she decided the florist was not aware of her husband's death. So she called to inform them that the roses probably should not be sent anymore.

To her surprise, the florist said, "Oh no, Mrs. Benny. Your husband set up a special fund before he died to keep the roses coming to you every day for as long as you live. He wanted you to know that his love was, indeed, undying."

The Last Petal

The days of love—

Like petals of a daisy—

I pull them off one by one

And toss them to eternity:

He loves me, he loves me not;

He loves me, he loves me not.

How will it all end?

What will the last petal say?

Canine Chaos

*C*ome with me to a spring night in Lawrence, Kansas. Take your seat in Hoch Auditorium and behold the Leipzig Gewandhaus Orchestra—the oldest continually operating orchestra in the world. The greatest composers and conductors in history have directed this orchestra. It was playing in the days of Beethoven (some of the musicians have been replaced).

You watch as stately dressed Europeans take their seats on the stage. You listen as professionals carefully tune their instruments. The percussionist puts her ear to the kettle drum. A violinist plucks the nylon string. A clarinet player tightens the reed. And you sit a bit straighter as the lights dim and the tuning stops. The music is about to begin.

The conductor, dressed in tails, strides onto the stage, springs onto the podium, and gestures for the orchestra to rise. You and two thousand others applaud. The musicians take their seats, the maestro takes his position, and the audience holds its breath.

There is a second of silence between lightning and thunder. And there is a second of silence between the raising of the baton and the explosion of the music. But when it falls, the heavens open and you are delightfully drenched in the downpour of Beethoven's *Third Symphony*.

Such was the power of that spring night in Lawrence, Kansas. That hot, spring night in Lawrence, Kansas. I mention the temperature so you'll understand why the doors were open. It was hot. Hoch Auditorium, a historic building, was not air-conditioned. Combine bright stage lights with formal dress and furious music, and the result is a heated orchestra. Outside doors on each side of the stage were left open in case of a breeze.

Enter, stage right, the dog. A brown, generic, Kansas dog. Not a mean dog. Not a mad dog. Just a curious dog. He passes between the double basses and makes his way through the second violins and into the cellos. His tail wags in beat with the music. As the dog passes between the players, they look at him, look at each other, and continue with the next measure.

The dog takes a liking to a certain cello. Perhaps it was the lateral passing of the bow. Maybe it was the eye-level view of the strings. Whatever it was, it caught the dog's attention, and he stopped and watched. The cellist wasn't sure what to do. He'd never played for a canine audience. And music schools don't teach you what dog slobber might do to the lacquer of a sixteenth-century Guarneri cello. But the dog did nothing but watch for a moment and then move on.

Had he passed on through the orchestra, the music might

have continued. Had he made his way across the stage into the motioning hands of a stagehand, the audience might never had noticed. But he didn't leave. He stayed. At home in the splendor. Roaming through the meadows of music.

He visited the woodwinds, turned his head at the trumpets, stepped between the flutists, and stopped by the side of the conductor. And Beethoven's *Third Symphony* came undone.

The musicians laughed. The audience laughed. The dog looked up at the conductor and panted. And the conductor lowered his baton.

The most historic orchestra in the world. One of the most moving pieces ever written. A night wrapped in glory, all brought to a stop by a wayward dog.

The chuckles ceased as the conductor turned. What fury might erupt? The audience grew quiet as the maestro faced them. What fuse had been lit? The polished, German director looked at the crowd, looked down at the dog, then looked back at the people, raised his hands in a universal gesture and . . . shrugged.

Everyone roared.

He stepped off the podium and scratched the dog behind the ears. The tail wagged again. The maestro spoke to the dog. He spoke in German, but the dog seemed to understand. The two visited for a few seconds before the maestro took his new friend by the collar and led him off the stage. You'd have thought the dog was Pavarotti the way the people applauded. The conductor returned and the music began and Beethoven seemed none the worse for the whole experience.

Can you find you and me in this picture?

I can. Just call us Fido. And consider God the Maestro.

And envision the moment when we will walk onto his stage. We won't deserve to. We will not have earned it. We may even surprise the musicians with our presence.

The music will be like none we've ever heard. We'll stroll among the angels and listen as they sing. We'll gaze at heaven's lights and gasp as they shine. And we'll walk next to the Maestro, stand by his side, and worship as he leads. . . . See the unseen and live for that event. [We are invited] to tune our ears to the song of the skies and long—long for the moment when we'll be at the Maestro's side.

He, too, will welcome. And he, too, will speak. But he will not lead us away. He will invite us to remain, forever his guests on his stage.

———

Erik Ketcherside
as told to Max Lucado
When God Whispers Your Name

Sam, the Garbage Man

🦢

Sam was the local garbage man. He was intellectually challenged, but he did his work with pride and care. He was a friendly, happy soul. He smiled and waved at people as he rode the garbage truck down the street. He talked to the children and petted the dogs. Everyone liked him.

Sam was a Christian, and he strove always to serve God in whatever ways he could. He often left notes on the garbage cans of the customers he served that said, "I'm Sam, your garbage man, and I love you."

One fall, the church Sam attended decided to have a week-long gospel meeting. They printed invitations for the members to hand out, and Sam was so excited. He left notes and invitations on all the garbage cans around the small town.

To the surprise and delight of the little congregation, half the town came, simply because Sam, the garbage man, had taken the time to invite them. And several people became Christians that week, simply because Sam, the garbage man, had loved them and taken the time to tell them so.

———

As told by Eldred Echols,
missionary to South Africa

Greyfriars Bobby

When my Christian vocal jazz group did a music outreach tour in Scotland, we were privileged to see an unusual memorial fountain and statue near Greyfriars Churchyard in Edinburgh. The statue and fountain honor a little dog named Greyfriars Bobby.

The little dog's master, a respected Scottish policeman, died and was buried in the churchyard. Everyone was touched to see Bobby standing watch over his master's grave at the funeral service. They were even more captivated by the dog's continued vigil for days and weeks and months to follow.

In fact, for the next five years little Bobby virtually lived on top of the tomb day and night. The Skye terrier left his master's side for only an hour at a time to visit his two admiring friends—the restaurant owner who fed him and the sexton who built a shelter for him at the stop. Strangely, on Saturdays, Bobby would wait for an extra dinner, which he kept for Sunday. He did not go for dinner on that day.

Word about the faithful little terrier's lifelong love, loyalty, and devotion to his master spread, and thousands of people from around the world visited the churchyard to see him standing watch, give him a little encouraging scratch behind the ear, or offer him a treat in praise.

When little Bobby finally died, too, his Scottish admirers—indeed, the entire country and beyond—paid tribute to him by burying him beside his master and erecting the memorial.

Don't you just hope that, when the time comes, you'll have been found as faithful and loyal to your Master?

From Scottish History

Love Is Stronger
Than Death

🕆

*L*ove is stronger than death. I know it's true because my grandmother has been gone for forty years, and I still love her. Death cannot erase her smile from my memory or mute her quiet whistling that I hear plainly in my mind. It can't remove the vivid image I have of her wearing her flour-sack smock and pleated bonnet as she walked up the little country lane to the mailbox.

Love is stronger than death. I know because I can still taste the special flavor of Grandmother's mashed potatoes. I can smell the sweet, delicious aroma of her butterscotch pie baking in the old farmhouse kitchen. Nobody else's tasted just like hers. I can still see the sticks of gum, candy canes, and tiny handmade yarn angels that hung on the cedar Christmas tree in the front room.

Love is stronger than death. So, I must learn to be content to know that love is not affected by death—it doesn't end; it doesn't diminish; it doesn't change. Instead, love is immortalized and eternalized through death. And the possibility of that love ever being damaged or broken is eliminated forever. I'll put my trust in love.

———

Mary Hollingsworth

Rainbows

Wedded Confusion

*Y*ou think things are confusing at your house? At New Philadelphia, Ohio, a double wedding was announced. A nineteen-year-old boy was to marry a sixteen-year-old girl. The groom's seventeen-year-old sister was to wed the father of the bride at the same time.

That means that the sister became her brother's mother-in-law, and the brother became his father-in-law's brother-in-law. His bride became her father's sister-in-law. And their children would be first cousins of the sister-in-law's mother-in-law.

Virgil Schense of Aberdeen, South Dakota, can even top that! He became his father's brother-in-law and the uncle of his three brothers and sisters. His three sisters became nieces of his wife and also her sisters-in-law. His wife became her sister's daughter-in-law's sister-in-law and also her husband's aunt.

Here's how things got that way: Virgil, son of his father's first wife, married the sister of his father's second wife.

"Ah, sweet mystery of life . . ."

Adapted from Lowell Thomas
Encyclopedia of 7700 Illustrations

I'll Be Seeing You

✝

$\mathcal{M}$y friend Lee Nelson is a funeral director for a prestigious chain of funeral homes in our area. One day he received a death call and went to pick up a deceased woman at a local hospital. The next day the woman's family came in to make arrangements for her funeral.

Lee described this family as "less than sophisticated" and related what happened as he was assisting them in making the final choices for their mother's service.

"Do you have an article of jewelry or clothing that you would like to have put on your mother during the service and then removed before the interment?" asked Lee.

Thinking for a moment, the daughter said, "Yes . . . yes I do." And she began digging around in her purse while Lee waited patiently.

Finally, she opened a small change purse and took something out, holding it out to Lee in her closed hand. Lee held out his hand, expecting to receive a necklace or some other piece of jewelry, but when he opened his hand, the dead woman's glass eye was staring at him.

Shocked and a little repulsed, Lee quietly put the glass eye down on the desk, stood up slowly, and said, "Would you please excuse me for a minute?" Then he left the room to try and recompose himself.

Out in the lobby of the funeral home, he related what had happened to his supervisor and the receptionist, and they all had a good laugh. Lee says it took him about ten minutes to regain his composure so he could go back into the office and help the family finish the arrangements.

He walked down the hall and had his hand on the office doorknob when his supervisor stopped him.

With a serious look on his face, he said, "Lee, did the family tell you what the mother's final words were?"

"No," said Lee.

"She said, 'I'll keep an eye out for you!'"

Lee said it took him another ten minutes to recover from that remark before he could face the family again and complete his task.

———

As told by H. Lee Nelson

Over in a Flash

$\mathcal{I}$t was Halloween night. Because they loved children and wanted to do something fun for them, Jeff and Connie decided to hand out candy at their door to the neighborhood kids. To add to the fun, Jeff wore a funny mask and gave the kids a little scare as they came to the door.

After a couple of hours of having fun and when the trick-or-treaters had slacked off, Connie decided to pull a little trick on Jeff. So she took off all her clothes and put on a trench coat. Then she sneaked out the back door, tiptoed around to the front of the house, crept up on the porch, and rang the doorbell.

Jeff, thinking it was more children, went to the door in his funny mask, yanked open the door, and yelled, "Booooo!"

Just as he yelled, Connie pulled open her trench coat and flashed her husband. Taken completely by surprise, and not realizing it was Connie, Jeff gasped and started backing away from the door. In his haste, he stumbled into the coffee table, tripped over it backward, and fell between the table and the sofa . . . breaking his leg.

That was the night that "trick or treat" took on a whole

new meaning to Jeff and Connie, and to this day they don't observe Halloween at their house. It's just too dangerous.

Teddy and Miss Thompson

$\mathcal{I}$ know of a schoolteacher named Miss Thompson. Every year, when she met her new students, she would say, "Boys and girls, I love you all the same. I have no favorites." Of course, she wasn't being completely truthful. Teachers do have favorites and, what is worse, most teachers have students that they just don't like.

Teddy Stallard was a boy that Miss Thompson just didn't like, and for good reason. He just didn't seem interested in school. There was a deadpan, blank expression on his face, and his eyes had a glassy, unfocused appearance. When she spoke to Teddy, he always answered in monosyllables. His clothes were musty, and his hair was unkempt. He wasn't an attractive boy, and he certainly wasn't likable.

Whenever she marked Teddy's papers, she got a certain perverse pleasure out of putting Xs next to the wrong answers, and when she put the Fs at the top of the papers, she always did it with a flair. She should have known better; she had Teddy's records, and she knew more about him than she wanted to admit. The records read this way:

1st Grade: Teddy shows promise with his work and attitude, but poor home situation.

2nd Grade: Teddy could do better. Mother is seriously ill. He receives little help at home.

3rd Grade: Teddy is a good boy, but too serious. He is a slow learner. His mother died this year.

4th Grade: Teddy is very slow, but well-behaved. His father shows no interest.

Christmas came and the boys and girls in Miss Thompson's class brought her Christmas presents. They piled their presents on her desk and crowded around to watch her open them. Among the presents, there was one from Teddy Stallard. She was surprised that he had brought her a gift. Teddy's gift was wrapped in brown paper and was held together with Scotch tape. On the paper were written the simple words, "For Miss Thompson from Teddy." When she opened Teddy's present, out fell a gaudy rhinestone bracelet, with half the stones missing, and a bottle of cheap perfume.

The other boys and girls began to giggle and smirk over Teddy's gifts, but Miss Thompson at least had enough sense to silence them by immediately putting on the bracelet and putting some of the perfume on her wrist. Holding her wrist up for the other children to smell, she said, "Doesn't it smell lovely?" And the children, taking their cue from the teacher, readily agreed with "oos" and "ahs."

At the end of the day, when school was over and the other children had left, Teddy lingered behind. He slowly came over to her desk and said softly, "Miss Thompson . . . Miss Thompson, you smell just like my mother . . . and her bracelet looks real pretty on you too. I'm glad you liked my presents."

When Teddy left, Miss Thompson got down on her knees and asked God to forgive her.

The next day when the children came to school, they were welcomed by a new teacher. Miss Thompson had become a different person. She was no longer just a teacher; she had become an agent of God. She was now a person committed to loving her children and doing things for them that would live on after her. She helped all the children, but especially the slow ones, and especially Teddy Stallard. By the end of that school year, Teddy showed dramatic improvement. He had caught up with most of the students and was even ahead of some.

She didn't hear from Teddy for a long time. Then one day, she received a note that read . . .

Dear Miss Thompson:

I wanted you to be the first to know. I will be graduating second in my class.

Love,

Teddy Stallard

Four years later, another note came:

Dear Miss Thompson:
They just told me I will be graduating first in my class. I wanted you to be the first to know. The university has not been easy, but I liked it.

Love,
Teddy Stallard

And, four years later:

Dear Miss Thompson:
As of today, I am Theodore Stallard, M.D. How about that? I wanted you to be the first to know. I am getting married next month, the 27th to be exact. I want you to come and sit where my mother would sit if she were alive. You are the only family I have now. Dad died last year.

Love,
Teddy Stallard

Miss Thompson went to that wedding and sat where Teddy's mother would have sat. She deserved to sit there; she had done something for Teddy that he could never forget.

Tony Campolo
Who Switched the Price Tags?

Hello, Mike

$\mathcal{P}$ reparing to build some bookshelves in my home office, I went to the local lumberyard in Monroe, Louisiana. As I waited for someone to assist me with which kind of lumber to buy and to get it cut to the proper length, I wandered around in the store at the front of the lumberyard.

"Hello Mike!" I heard a crusty voice say nearby.

I looked around but saw no one. So I assumed someone had just said it in passing. Then I heard it again.

"Hello, Mike!"

I glanced around and caught the eye of the clerk at the counter, who grinned and said, "It's the parrot in the cage in the middle of the store, ma'am. His name is Mike. He's wanting you to talk to him."

"Oh," I said skeptically and walked around the end of the hardware aisle to find a giant birdcage sitting on a stand. Inside was an ebony black myna bird.

"Hello, Mike!" he said, looking at me and walking back and forth on his perch and nodding his head up and down.

"Hello, Mike," I said, a little embarrassed by the whole thing.

"Stick 'em up! This is a holdup!" he croaked.

I laughed and said, "Okay, you've got me." And I lifted my hands.

"Put your arms down. You're losing friends!" he joked.

For the next three or four minutes Mike and I had a conversation—you know, all the standard stuff you say to a parrot: "Polly want a cracker? Here kitty, kitty." And the like.

Then suddenly Mike quit talking. He went stone silent, no matter how hard I tried to coax him, he said nothing. I repeated every stupid bird sentence I could remember. Nothing. He just sat there looking at me.

Finally, after I'd made a total idiot of myself and started to walk away, Mike said, loud enough for the whole world to hear, "Silly, birds can't talk!" Then he cackled with glee like a two-pound hen that just laid a three-pound egg.

That was the last conversation I've had with a bird.

I Pledge Allegiance

*C*aptain John S. McCain, a retired U.S. Navy officer and a U.S. senator from Arizona, who, at this writing, is running for president in the 2000 elections, spent five and one-half years as a prisoner of war during the Vietnam War. During the early years of his imprisonment, the North Vietnamese Army kept him and his comrades either in solitary confinement or with only two or three prisoners in a cell.

In 1971 McCain was moved out of isolation into a large room with thirty or forty other prisoners. Captain McCain says this was a wonderful change that came about because of the efforts of millions of Americans on behalf of the POWs.

One of the men moved into the room with McCain was named Mike Christian. Mike came from a small town near Selma, Alabama, where he lived with his rather poor family. In fact, Mike didn't even wear a pair of shoes until he was about thirteen years old.

At age seventeen, Mike enlisted in the U.S. Navy. He later earned a commission by going to Officer Training School. Still later, he became a Naval Flight Officer and was assigned to the Vietnam conflict where he was eventually shot down and captured in 1967. Mike had a keen appreciation for the opportunities America and her military provide for people who want to work and succeed.

As part of the improved treatment by the Vietnamese, some prisoners were allowed to receive packages from home. Some of these packages yielded small items of clothing, such as handkerchiefs and scarves. From these items, and using a bamboo needle he found, Mike created an American flag, which he sewed onto the inside of his shirt.

Every afternoon, before they ate their standard bowl of soup, the American prisoners would hang Mike's shirt on the wall of the cell and, with their hands over their hearts, they would sincerely repeat the Pledge of Allegiance. The Pledge of Allegiance may not seem like the most important part of our day now, but in that stark, dank cell, it was indeed a most important and meaningful event.

One day the Vietnamese searched the Americans' cell, as they did periodically. They discovered Mike's shirt with Old Glory sewn inside and removed it. That evening they returned, opened the cell door, and beat Mike Christian severely for the next couple of hours in front of Captain McCain and the other prisoners. Then they threw him back inside the cell and locked the door.

"We cleaned Mike's wounds as best we could," said Captain McCain, "and helped him onto the concrete slab in the middle of the cell on which we slept."

A while later, after the excitement had died down, McCain

looked over to where they had laid Mike, but he was gone. Dusk had settled on the camp, so the cell was dark, and it was difficult to see. There were only four small, dim light bulbs in the large room, one in each corner.

Finally, Captain McCain's eyes found Mike. He had painfully braced himself up in the corner under one of the dim lights. His eyes were swollen almost shut from the beating they had given him. And blood was oozing from around the make-do bandages they had tied around his head and arms. There, with a piece of red cloth, another shirt, and his bamboo needle, Mike Christian was slowly making another American flag.

Captain McCain said the other prisoners asked each other, "Why? Why is he doing it? The Vietnamese will just find it too, sooner or later. And next time, they might kill him." Mike wasn't making the flag because it made him feel better. He was making the flag because he knew how important it was to the other Americans to be able to pledge their allegiance to their flag and homeland. And, indeed, those Americans never took the Pledge of Allegiance for granted again.

———

Retold from a speech by Captain John S. McCain

The Pledge of Allegiance

I pledge allegiance to the flag of the United States of America and to the republic for which it stands, one nation under God, indivisible, with liberty and justice for all.

Softball and Singing

$\mathcal{I}$t was during the summer of 1979, and a blistering summer it was in the humid swamps of Louisiana. The church softball team had made it to the finals in the city championships, primarily because of one man—Pete, the pitcher. And almost the entire church turned out to the see the championship game against the Bulldogs sponsored by the Bayou Trucking Company.

As we were sitting in the bleachers waiting for the game to begin, I began thinking back on the unusual events that led us to this time and place. And as Pete walked out onto the pitcher's mound, I smiled to myself, remembering.

Pete was not a churchgoing man. He hadn't been to church in over thirty years. Someone in the church had criticized him unfairly one time, and he had never come back.

However, Pete's wife, Joan, had faithfully continued to come to church and worship God all through the years. She came alone most times now, since the kids were grown, but she always came. She was so dedicated to the church, in fact, that she had taken the job as church secretary at a much lower salary than she could have earned elsewhere.

In 1976 my husband and I moved to Louisiana to minister with the church where Joan was secretary. During those three years we had become close friends with Joan and her children, who were also members of the church. We had even gotten to know Pete to some degree at picnics and other outings.

My husband was a song leader, and a good one. He loved to sing, and other people loved to sing with him. So one of the first things he began to do at the new church was to try and help improve the singing. He did that by having singing practice each Sunday evening for an hour just prior to the Sunday evening worship time.

Joan told us that there were two things that Pete loved to do. One was to play softball; the other was to sing. So my husband called Pete one day and invited him to come sing with us on Sunday evenings. Although he sounded some-what interested, he didn't come. We kept hoping he would change his mind, but months went by, and he never came.

Some of the older men at the church knew Pete from days gone by and tried to build bridges to him, but to no avail. Finally, some of the younger men decided to form a softball team and compete in the city league. When they did, one of the older men told them they should ask Pete to play because he was an excellent pitcher. So one of the team captains called Pete and, to our delight, he agreed to play with them.

After several months of playing softball and eating out with the church team and their spouses, Pete began to warm up a little. And one Sunday evening, unannounced, Pete walked into singing practice with Joan. She was grinning from ear to ear. However, as soon as singing practice was over, Pete left. He did not, as we had hoped, stay for worship.

Every week after that for several months Pete came to sing and then left. He had a beautiful bass voice and read music very well. It was obvious he loved the singing, and he enjoyed playing softball with the guys from the church, but that was it.

This routine went on for two years. Then one Sunday evening, out of the blue, Pete didn't leave after singing practice. He stayed for the worship service. And every Sunday night after that, he stayed.

Still, Pete had never really set things right in his heart with the Lord for all the years he had ignored him. Joan, as faithful in prayer as in service, continued to pray for Pete, as did we all.

As summer came to a close and softball season was nearing its end, our team was in first place. Pete had pitched his heart out throughout this second season, and the rest of the team had worked just as hard. We had one game to go to win the city championship.

The Sunday morning before the final game dawned clear, humid, and hot, as usual. And, as usual, we went to church. The singing was especially beautiful that morning, and the church was in good spirits. As the thoughtful sermon came to a close, and my husband began the final song, the doors in the back opened, and Pete walked slowly and humbly down the aisle to the front.

There wasn't a dry eye in the place that day. So many of us were laughing and crying, in fact, that the song almost stopped.

Pete and the Lord got back on good terms that day. It wasn't because of some Bible-slapping sermon. It wasn't because Pete's wife tormented him into it. It wasn't because he had a supernatural encounter with an angel. It was simply because of softball and singing with a group of dedicated Christians.

And now, here we were sitting in the bleachers at the softball field watching our brother Pete warm up. And that smile crept across my face again.

We won, by the way.

Brother John

✝

*E*veryone just called him "Brother John." He was a small, gentle man with quiet words and twinkling smiles, but John Knox was a real, live hero to many of us.

The doctor had told this eighty-year-old man that his heart was growing weak and it was necessary for him to walk daily. So every morning he walked with the sunrise from his home across town to the local hospital. Rain or shine, cold or hot, he trudged the six long miles. It was his "heart walk," he said.

At the hospital information desk, he made a list of all the people who were members of our church. Then he went from room to room visiting. If a patient needed a newspaper, Brother John went downstairs and bought them a paper. If they needed a cup of coffee, he went to the nurses' station and asked if it was all right for them to have it; then he went to the cafeteria and got it for them . . . with his own money. If they wanted him to read to them, he read; pray with them, he prayed; talk to them, he talked. He tried to meet whatever immediate need they had.

Brother John didn't stay long when he came to visit. He

only came to help. If help was needed, he stayed. If it wasn't, he moved on to others who might need him. The doctors and nurses in the hospital came to respect and admire Brother John for his quiet service and gentle care of their patients. And they grew to anticipate his daily visits with appreciation for they saw the smiles and peace he left behind.

One of the local service organizations awarded Brother John a plaque as "Humanitarian of the Year." He was so pleased. When it came time to accept the award, though, Brother John just blushed shyly and said, "I really did it just for me. It was my heart walk, you know." And everyone knew that it was, indeed, a walk of his heart.

———

Mary Hollingsworth

Rainbows

The Good, the True, the Fair

Where'er I find the Good, the True, the Fair,
I ask no names—God's spirit dwelleth there!

———

Samuel Taylor Coleridge

The Secret

$\mathcal{S}$ir William Osler, the famous English physician, was visiting one of London's leading children's hospitals and noticed that all the children in a certain ward were playing together at one end of the room, except for a little tiny girl. Susan sat forlornly on the edge of her high, narrow hospital bed, clutching an inexpensive doll. Sir William looked at the lonely little girl and then quizzed the ward nurse.

"We've tried to get Susan to play with the other kids," the nurse whispered, "but the other children just won't have anything to do with her. You see, no one ever comes to see her. Her mother is dead, and her father has been here just once—he brought her that doll. The children have a strange code. Visitors mean so much. If you don't have any visitors, you are ignored."

With a crooked smile on his wise, old face, Sir William walked over to the child's bed and asked loudly enough for the other children to hear, "Susan, may I sit down, please?"

The little girl's eyes lit up as she nodded.

"I can't stay very long this visit," the doctor went on, "but I have wanted to see you so badly."

For five minutes he sat talking with her, even inquiring about her doll's health and solemnly pulling out his stethoscope to listen to the doll's chest. As he finally left, he turned to the bright-eyed little girl and said loudly, "You won't forget our secret, will you? And mind you, don't tell anyone."

At the door he looked back. His new little friend was now the center of a curious and admiring throng of children. And he smiled, knowing that special attention can cure a multitude of childhood maladies.

Rules for Teachers

*Y*ou think teachers now have it hard? Consider these rules for teachers from the oldest wooden schoolhouse in St. Augustine, Florida, dated 1872, and count your blessings!

1. Teachers each day will fill the lamps and clean their chimneys.
2. Each teacher will bring a bucket of water and scuttle of coal for the day's session.
3. Make your pens carefully. You may whittle nibs to the individual taste of the pupils.
4. Men teachers may take one evening a week for courting purposes, or two evenings a week if they go to church regularly.
5. After ten hours in school, the teacher may spend the rest of the time reading the Bible or other good books.
6. Women teachers who marry or engage in unseemly conduct will be dismissed.
7. Every teacher should lay aside from each day's pay a goodly sum of his earnings for his benefit during his

declining years so that he will not become a burden on society.

8. Any teacher who smokes, uses liquor in any form, frequents pool or public halls, or gets shaved in a barber shop will give good reason to suspect his worth, intention, integrity, and honesty.

9. The teacher who performs his labor faithfully and without fault for five years will be given an increase of twenty-five cents per week in his pay, providing the Board of Education approves.

Teacher! Teacher!

$\mathcal{A}$ little girl in the first grade came running into the classroom one day during recess and clamored, "Teacher! Teacher! Two boys are fighting out on the playground, and I think the one on the bottom would really like to see you!"

Who Are You?

✦

"Who are you?" asked the Caterpillar.

Alice replied, rather shyly, "I hardly know, sir, just at present. At least I know who I was when I got up this morning, but then I think I must have changed several times since then."

"What do you mean by that?" said the Caterpillar sternly. "Explain yourself!"

"I can't explain myself, I'm afraid, sir," said Alice, "because I'm not myself, you see."

"I don't see," said the Caterpillar.

"I'm afraid I can't put it more clearly," Alice replied very politely, "for I can't understand it myself, to begin with, and being so many different sizes in a day is very confusing."

———

Lewis Carroll

Alice's Adventures in Wonderland

As Close as You Can Get

$\mathcal{D}$uring one of the many moves my family made, the moving van transporting my parents' household goods and lifelong treasures flipped over and burned in the middle of the Dallas–Fort Worth Turnpike. Most of their household goods were lost in the fire.

For years after that, Mom would miss some kitchen utensil or another item and say, "I guess we lost that in the fire." Even that she bore with grace and smiles.

About three years ago we celebrated my parents' sixtieth wedding anniversary. We had a nice luncheon at a restaurant with our immediate family and a couple of close friends. As is our family's nature, we told a lot of funny stories and relived meaningful times together. It was a joyous occasion.

The admiration that my dad has for my mother is obvious, sincere, and deep. And my mother feels the same way about him. They are a mutual admiration society of two. That admiration is based on their individual and joint relationships with God, who has always been a vital and integral part of their marriage and our family—a foretaste of heaven on earth. So I finally asked them to tell us to what they attributed their long, happy marriage.

My dad said, "Well, I know there's no such thing as a perfect wife, but your mother is as close as any woman could ever get. She's followed me around all over the country and never complained. She's done everything a wife and mother is supposed to do and a lot more. She's the reason we've had a long, happy marriage."

As usual, my mother just smiled with shy embarrassment and said nothing. After all, what more was there to say? Dad had said it all.

The Hans Shroud Story

World War II was raging in Europe, and things were not going well. The Allied forces had been taking a severe beating outside Paris, France, for several days. At last one bright, crisp morning, an Allied spy reported to the Allied general that he had located the enemy headquarters. He took the general to the edge of a cliff and pointed to its location.

The general called for the regiment's top gunner—a soldier named Hans Shroud. He led Shroud to the edge of the cliff.

"Corporal, do you see that valley across the way?" asked the general.

"Yes sir!" snapped the corporal in crisp military fashion.

"Do you see the clump of trees about halfway back on the right side of the valley?"

"Yes sir!"

"Can you make out a small, white house inside that group of trees?"

"Yes sir!"

"That has been confirmed as the enemies' headquarters. Do you think you can hit that house, corporal?"

"Yes sir," said the corporal quietly.

"Then get to it!"

"Yes sir!" saluted the corporal, taking his leave.

With help from his regiment, Corporal Shroud brought the giant gun to the cliff's edge. He made careful calculations as to the trajectory of the shot. Then he loaded the gun, lined up the sights, and fired. The shot was accurate. The little white house exploded into thousands of flaming pieces that shot into the air and through the grove of trees.

"You did it! You did it!" shouted the general excitedly. "That was excellent shooting, son. Excellent shooting!"

"Thank you, sir," said the corporal quietly.

"You'll get a medal for this, my boy!"

As the general slapped the corporal on the back and congratulated him, he noticed that tears were running down the young man's face.

"I don't understand, son," said the crusty old general. "You may have just saved the entire war for the Allied forces. You should be elated. Why are you crying?"

"That house—the one I just blew up—belonged to my parents, sir. They still live there. The enemy had to have taken it over by force. I've just killed the family I love to save the country I love."

Love sometimes demands great sacrifice.

From World War II Records

Life's Harmonies

Ella Wheeler Wilcox
Poems of Power

Let no man pray that he know not sorrow,
    Let no soul ask to be free from pain,
For the gall of today is the sweet of tomorrow,
    And the moment's loss is the lifetime's gain.

Through want of a thing does its worth redouble,
    Through hunger's pangs does the feast content,
And only the heart that has harbored trouble,
    Can fully rejoice when joy is sent.

Let no man shrink from the bitter tonics
    Of grief, and yearning, and need, and strife,
For the rarest chords in the soul's harmonies
    Are found in the minor strains of life.

Stay in the Race

When they began working on the movie *Ben Hur*, Cecil B. DeMille, the director, talked to Charlton Heston—star of the great epic—about the all-important chariot race at the end of the movie. He decided Heston should actually learn to drive the chariot himself, rather than just using a stunt double. Heston, always the professional, agreed to take chariot-driving lessons to make the movie as authentic as possible.

Learning to drive a chariot with horses four abreast, however, was no small matter. After extensive work and days of practice, Heston returned to the movie set and reported in to DeMille.

"I think I can drive the chariot all right, Cecil," said Heston, "but I'm not at all sure I can actually win the race."

Smiling slightly, DeMille said, "Heston, you just stay in the race, and I'll make sure you win."

Isn't it amazing how much DeMille sounds like God talking to us?

As reported by Charlton Heston

It's a Girl!

*J*ack became a Christian on Sunday. On Wednesday afternoon his wife, Carol, gave birth to a beautiful baby girl. Jack, a big, burly guy who had a gruff voice and flamboyant manner, was thrilled. And he wanted to tell somebody.

The church met on Wednesday evening for Bible study. So, being excited about his new daughter and his new church family at the same time, naturally Jack thought we would all want to hear the good news.

There was a side entrance to the auditorium where the adult class met. When you came in that door, you were standing in front of the congregation for all to see. Ron, the local minister, had just stood up to begin the Bible study when Jack burst in the side door beaming and announced for all the world to hear, "It's a girl!"

There were a few muffled giggles, but everyone basically reacted happily. Then Jack bounced past Ron and politely hoisted himself up to sit on top of the communion table, bringing shocked gasps from the conservative group in the rear of the room. Jack, never having been a churchgoer before, was oblivious to his religious faux pas and proceeded to give us an exuberant blow-by-blow account of the day's events. Meanwhile, Ron, a highly dignified, white-shirt-and-navy-suit kind of minister, was quickly turning ashen, not quite knowing how to stop Jack politely.

To top off his big announcement, Jack hopped down off the "holy" table and bounded up and down the aisles, handing out cigars to all the men and candy to all the ladies in the congregation. The first cigar went, of course, to Ron, whose face instantly flushed from ashen to scarlet. And the gasps from the back erupted and lapsed into mortified silence. I collapsed in laughter on the second pew.

Then, as suddenly as he had burst into the room, Jack was gone. He went back to the hospital to be with Carol and Super Baby. He didn't even stay for Bible study.

When the guffaws and gasps died down, the old ladies on the back pew stopped sucking air, and I got my breath, I glanced up to see Ron still standing in front of the class with his Bible in one hand and the cigar in the other. His feet were frozen in place, and he couldn't, for the life of him, figure out what to say. Finally, with obvious fluster and fumbling, he stuck the cigar in his inside coat pocket and said, "I'll just put this away so no one will smoke it."

At that point I lost it completely, so I escaped to the ladies' room where I went into hysterics. I'm sure the Good Lord was laughing too. And the Scripture skipped through my mind that says, "Rejoice with those who rejoice."

Way to go, Jack. Thanks for loosening our spiritual ties a bit.

Destiny and Wisdom

 estiny came down to an island, centuries ago, and summoned three of the inhabitants before him.

"What would you do," asked Destiny, "if I told you that tomorrow the island will be completely inundated by an immense tidal wave?"

The first man, who was a cynic, said, "Why, I would eat, drink, and carouse, and make love all night long!"

The second man, who was a mystic, said, "I would go to the sacred grove with my loved ones and make sacrifices to the gods and pray without ceasing."

And the third man, who loved reason, thought for a while, confused and troubled, and said, "Why, I would assemble our wisest men and begin at once to study how to live underwater."

Leo Rosten

Captain Newman, M.D.

Who's Doing This?

$\mathcal{H}$e was only five years old, but he had a big, booming voice with which he would, no doubt, become a preacher, or so his mother thought. He was the light of her life.

He was to be the ring bearer in the wedding, including tux, tails, and satin pillow. It was a dubious honor in his young opinion, but since he had to do it, he was totally in control of the situation.

Rehearsal went well, except that his mother thought he was walking a bit too fast down the aisle. At the wedding the next night his mother positioned herself about halfway down the bridal path on the seat next to the aisle so she could encourage her son to slow down.

As expected, when the procession started, his mother decided that Junior was moving too fast. Just as he got to her pew, she put her hand out and whispered, "Slow down, sweetheart."

Insulted by the insinuation, Junior stopped midaisle, laid the satin pillow on the floor, backed off from his mother, put his little hands on his hips, and boomed, "Look here, woman! Who's doing this—me or you?"

The audience rippled with laughter, and his mother slid down into her pew, totally humiliated. Junior calmly straightened his little tux jacket, picked up the satin pillow, and solemnly marched to his appointed place at the front of the church. The rest of the wedding was, in comparison, uneventful.

———

Mary Hollingsworth

A Few Hallelujahs for Your Ho Hums

Open-Minded

Sam didn't really *intend* to be a troublemaker; it just sort of turned out that way. The truth is, he was so bright that most teachers couldn't stay ahead of him; his active little mind looked around for something to occupy itself, and he often ended up in mischief.

On one of those occasions, two frustrated teachers brought Sam by the ear in search of the supervisor, who was also frustrated. The supervisor thought it the better part of wisdom to ask Louis, a weightlifter and fellow teacher, to discuss the problem with Sam.

The supervisor could hear the rather rambunctious discussion, and soon Sam emerged rubbing his painful sitting-down place and returned to his classroom much more subdued. Louis followed him out of the "conference room," which doubled as the janitor's closet.

"Louis, how'd it go with Sam?" asked the supervisor.

"Oh, he's much more open-minded about the situation now," said Louis. "I opened it from the other end!"

Like Sam, sometimes we just need to be a little more open-minded about things.

Don't You Recognize Me?

A Jewish boy, who suffered under the Nazis in World War II, was living in a small Polish village when he and all the other Jews of the vicinity were rounded up by Nazi SS troops and sentenced to death. This boy joined his neighbors in digging a shallow ditch for their graves, then faced the firing squad with his parents.

Sprayed with machine-gun fire, bodies fell into the ditch, and the Nazis covered the crumpled bodies with dirt. But none of the bullets hit the little boy. He was splattered with the blood of his parents, and when they fell into the ditch, he pretended to be dead and fell on top of them. The grave was so shallow that the covering of dirt did not prevent his breathing.

Several hours later, when darkness fell, he clawed his way out of the grave. With blood and dirt caked to his little body, he made his way to the nearest house and begged for help. Recognizing him as one of the Jewish boys marked for death, house after house turned him away as people feared getting into trouble with the SS troops.

Then something inside seemed to guide him to say something that was very strange for a Jewish boy to say. When the next family responded to his timid knocking in the still of the night, they heard him cry, "Don't you recognize me? I am the Jesus you say you love."

After a poignant pause, the woman who stood in the doorway swept him into her arms and kissed him. From that day on, the members of that family cared for the boy as though he was one of their own.

———

Tony Campolo

Who Switched the Price Tags?

The Excellent Man

*C*ripple him, and you have a Sir Walter Scott.

Lock him in a prison cell, and you have a John Bunyan.

Bury him in the snows of Valley Forge, and you have a George Washington.

Raise him in abject poverty, and you have an Abraham Lincoln.

Subject him to bitter religious prejudice, and you have a Disraeli.

Strike him down with infantile paralysis, and he becomes a Franklin D. Roosevelt.

Burn him so severely in a schoolhouse fire that the doctors say he will never walk again, and you have a Glenn Cunningham, who set the world's record in 1934 for running a mile in four minutes and 6.7 seconds.

Deafen a genius composer, and you have a Ludwig van Beethoven.

Have him or her born black in a society filled with racial discrimination, and you have a Booker T. Washington, a George Washington Carver, or a Martin Luther King Jr.

Make him the first child to survive in a poor Italian family of eighteen children, and you have an Enrico Caruso.

Have him born of parents who survived a Nazi concentration camp, paralyze him from the waist down when he is four, and you have the incomparable concert violinist, Itzhak Perlman.

Call him a slow learner, "retarded," and write him off as ineducable, and you have an Albert Einstein.

———

Ted Engstrom

The Pursuit of Excellence

Ready to Take the Bridge

$\mathcal{M}$y husband and I ministered with a church in Pittsburgh, Pennsylvania, in the early 1970s. During the time we were living there, a major bridge was under construction across one of the three large rivers that come together in Pittsburgh (thus the name of their famous sports arena, Three Rivers Stadium).

This bridge was to be a primary thoroughfare from one side of the river to the other, ending in the downtown area. It was extremely high, perhaps eighty or ninety feet above the river, in order to allow for river traffic beneath it.

The bridge was about half finished when the funds for its completion were cut off. So, for the next few years, this massive bridge stretched out to the middle of the river and just stopped.

Officials in the area, concerned for public safety, put up barricades, brightly colored warning signs, and lights to keep people from accidentally driving onto the bridge. Still, in spite of their best efforts, a few people managed to get onto the bridge. A few desperate people even used the bridge as a place to commit suicide by driving their cars off the bridge and into the river far below.

As a result, when people in that region were really frustrated, had a bad day, or were feeling emotionally desperate and wanted to express their total exasperation, they would often say, "I'm about ready to take the bridge." And guess which bridge they meant!

The bridge was finally completed, but the phrase remains as a monument to it in the minds of older Pittsburgh citizens even today.

Saint George and the Dragon

$\mathcal{A}$ tramp was looking for a handout one day in a picturesque old English village. Hungry almost to the point of fainting, he stopped by a pub bearing the classic name "Inn of St. George and the Dragon."

"Please, ma'am, could you spare me a bite to eat?" he asked the lady who answered his knock at the kitchen door.

"A bite to eat?" she growled. "For a sorry, no-good bum—a foul-smelling beggar? No!" she snapped as she almost slammed the door on his hand.

Halfway down the lane the tramp stopped, turned around, and eyed the words "St. George and the Dragon." He went back and knocked again on the kitchen door.

"Now what do you want?" the woman asked angrily.

"Well, ma'am, if Saint George is in, may I speak with him this time?"

David Augsburger
The Freedom of Forgiveness

Courage, Old Boy

The party aboard ship was in full swing. Speeches were being made by the captain, the crew, and the guests enjoying the weeklong voyage. Sitting at the head table was a seventy-year-old man who, somewhat embarrassed, was doing his best to accept the praise being poured on him.

Earlier that morning a young woman had apparently fallen overboard, and within seconds this elderly gentleman was in the cold, dark waters at her side. The woman was rescued, and the elderly man became an instant hero.

When time finally came for the brave passenger to speak, the stateroom fell into a hush as he rose from his chair. He went to the microphone and, in what was probably the shortest hero's speech ever offered, spoke these stirring words: "I just want to know one thing—who pushed me?"

Ted Engstrom

Motivation to Last a Lifetime

A Good Question

$\mathcal{A}$ man was once hit on the head and fell into a deep coma. He stayed there for a very long time. People thought he was dead, so they sent him to a funeral home and stuck him in a coffin. At two o'clock in the morning, all alone in this dimly lit room, he sat up and looked around.

"Good night!" he said. "What's going on? If I'm alive, why am I in a casket? And, if I'm dead, why do I have to go to the bathroom?"

———

Harry S. Truman

A Tinker's Bill

✝

*H*enry Ford once hired a man named Charlie Steinmetz to build some huge electric generators to run the first Ford Motor plant in Dearborn, Michigan. Some people would have thought Steinmetz was an unlikely candidate for such a job since he was a dwarf and terribly deformed. Yet, what Charlie lacked in physical ability, he made up in mental ability. He was a genius with electricity.

When the big plant suddenly came to a screeching halt one day for no apparent reason, Ford called in all his best mechanics, but they could find no solution. Finally, he called Charlie Steinmetz and asked him to come and find the problem. Charlie fiddled with this, tinkered with that, rewired a couple of things, and flipped the master switch. And shortly, everything was fixed, and the generators were running again.

A few days later, Ford received an invoice from Steinmetz for ten thousand dollars. He was shocked at the amount and refused to pay so much for such a seemingly small amount of work. He wrote a letter to his friend Charlie and included the unpaid bill. The note said, "Charlie: It seems awfully steep, this $10,000, for a man who for just a little while tinkered around with a few motors."

Mr. Steinmetz revised his invoice and sent it back to Ford with this note: "Henry: For tinkering around with motors, $10; for knowing *where* to tinker, $9,990." Ford paid the invoice without further comment.

Speaking of Electricity

🦅

An elementary teacher gave her young class an in-school writing assignment. They were to choose a famous person and write the story of that person's life.

Not wanting to spend an undue amount of time on the assignment, here's what little Jerry wrote about Benjamin Franklin:

Benjamin Franklin was born in Boston. He grew up and moved to Philadelphia. He became a scientist. One day he met a woman on the street. He married her and discovered electricity. The end.

———

Clyde Shrode

Chirpy

$\mathcal{A}$ newspaper in San Diego printed the story of a woman who had a little canary whom she affectionately named Chirpy. The little bird brought all kinds of song and beauty into their home.

One day, while vacuuming, she thought, *My, the bottom of Chirpy's cage is dirty. I'll just vacuum the bottom of his cage.*

While she was vacuuming, the phone rang. So when she reached over for the phone, she lifted up the vacuum cleaner and it sucked in Chirpy, all the way down the tube, down to the little bag. Of course, she opened the vacuum cleaner and cut the bag open and there was Chirpy inside trying to survive. She breathed a sigh of relief. But she thought, *Oh, he's so dirty.* So she put him under a faucet and ran water all over him. And then when she finished with him under the faucet, where he was about to drown, she dried him with a blow-dryer.

A newspaper reporter asked, "Well, what's he like now?"

She replied, "Well, he doesn't sing very much anymore."

———

Max Lucado
In the Eye of the Storm

Up in the Air

✢

$\mathcal{A}$ fellow named George owned an apartment complex and had just completed the exterior brickwork on the second floor. He had some bricks left over and was trying to decide the best way to get the load of bricks back down to ground level without breaking them. He noticed a fifty-five-gallon barrel on the ground and thought, *I know what I'll do. I'll tie some rope around that barrel, hook a pulley to the second-floor eave, and pull the barrel up to the second floor. Then I can load the bricks into the barrel and let it back down to the ground.*

So that's what he began to do. He tied the rope around the barrel, ran it over the pulley on the second floor, and pulled the barrel up to the second-story level. Then he tied the rope to the root of a nearby tree. He went up to the second floor balcony and loaded the bricks into the barrel. Then he went back downstairs, grabbed the rope and pulled it loose from the root.

Now, folks, that fifty-five-gallon drum full of bricks was four times heavier than George. So the barrel shot down lickety-split, and George shot up lickety-split. And you know what happened. As George shot past the barrel, it hit his shoulder, slammed against his hip, and whomped his knee-cap. The barrel crashed to the ground, and George's head smashed into the pulley above, cracking his skull. There he was, dangling by the rope from the second-story roof.

When the barrel hit the ground, the bricks were so heavy they knocked the bottom out of the barrel. So now George was heavier than the barrel. Yep! Down he went, and up it came. This time, the barrel caught him on the other side. It whomped his other knee, scraped past his other hip, broke his nose, and dumped him on top of the pile of leftover bricks below. He turned both ankles, scuffed up his shins, and the corners of the bricks punched him in the side. So George let out a yell and turned loose of the rope.

You guessed it. Now the barrel was four times heavier than the rope, so it came bombing down on top of George to finish the job from the previous hit-and-run. And George found himself lying in the hospital, bruised, sprained, and broken, saying to himself, *I don't know whether to file one insurance claim or five. . . .*

I think most of us sometimes feel like George. Life has dumped us bruised, sprained, and broken on its pile of left-overs. We're all whomped up and don't think we can even get up and walk away. That's just the nature of the way things happen in this life. Things do go wrong. Everything is always up in the air, at least here on earth!

————

Paul Faulkner

Making Things Right When Things Go Wrong

Opportunity

I am the blind man you pass on the street

Selling my papers for something to eat;

I am the beggar who knocks on your door

Pleading a morsel or crumb—nothing more.

I am the hitchhiker shivering, cold,

Thumbing a ride with cumbersome load;

I am the widow whose loneliness cries

To have happy laughter to drown out my sighs.

I am the cripple whose arthritic hand

Reaches to touch you. Can you understand?

I am the infant whose parents have fled,

Caring not whether I'm living or dead.

I am the homeless, rejected and poor;

Hear with your heart my lonely adjure:

Lend me your comfort, share your kind smile,

Just linger a moment or chat for a while.

The Captive Outfielder

The boy was filled with anxiety that seemed to concentrate in his stomach, giving him a sense of tightness there, as if knotted up into a ball that would never come undone again. He had his violin under his chin, and before him was the music stand. On the walls of the studio, the pictures of the great musicians were frowning upon him in massive disapproval. Right behind him was a portrait of Paganini, who positively glowered down at the boy, full of malevolence and impatience.

That, said the boy to himself, *is because he could really play the violin, and I can't and never will be able to. And he knows it and thinks I'm a fool.*

Below Paganini was a portrait of Mozart in profile. He had a white wig tied neatly at the back with a bow of black ribbon. Mozart should have been looking straight ahead, but his left eye, which was the only one visible, seemed to be turned a little watching the boy. The look was one of disapproval. When Mozart was the boy's age—that is, ten—he had already composed several pieces and could play the violin and the organ. Mozart didn't like the boy either.

147

On the other side of the Paganini portrait was the blocky face of Johann Sebastian Bach. It was a grim face, bleak with disappointment. Whenever the boy was playing, it seemed to him that Johann Sebastian Bach was shaking his head in resigned disapproval of his efforts. There were other portraits around the studio—Beethoven, Brahms, Chopin. Not one of them was smiling. They were all in agreement that this boy was certainly the poorest kind of musician and never would learn his instrument, and it was painful to them to have to listen to him while he had his lesson.

Of all these great men of music who surrounded him, the boy hated Johann Sebastian Bach the most. This was because his teacher, Mr. Olinsky, kept talking about Bach as if without Bach there never would have been any music. Bach was like a god to Mr. Olinsky, and he was a god the boy could never hope to please.

"All right," said Mr. Olinsky, who was at the grand piano. "'The Arioso.' And you will kindly remember the time. Without time no one can play the music of Johann Sebastian Bach." Mr. Olinsky exchanged glances with the portrait of Bach, and the two seemed in perfect agreement with each other. The boy was quite sure they carried on disheartened conversations about him after his lesson.

There was a chord from the piano. The boy put the bow to the string and started. But it was no good. At the end of the second bar, Mr. Olinsky took his hands from the piano and covered his face with them and shook his head, bending over the keyboard. Bach shook his head too. In the awful silence, all the portraits around the studio expressed their disapproval, and the boy felt more wretched than ever and not too far removed from tears.

"The *time*," said Mr. Olinsky eventually. "The time. Take that first bar. What is the value of the first note?"

"A quarter note," said the boy.

"And the next note?"

"A sixteenth."

"Good. So you have one quarter note and four sixteenth notes making a bar of two quarters. Not so?"

"Yes."

"But the first quarter note is tied to the first sixteenth note. They are the same note. So the first note, which is C sharp, is held for five sixteenths, and then the other three sixteenths follow. Not so?"

"Yes," said the boy.

"Then why don't you play it that way?"

To this the boy made no reply. The reason he didn't play it that way was that he couldn't play it that way. It wasn't fair to have a quarter note and then tie it to a sixteenth note. It was just a dirty trick like Grasshopper Smith pulled when he was pitching in the Little League. Grasshopper Smith was on the Giants, and the boy was on the Yankees. The Grasshopper always retained the ball for just a second after he seemed to have thrown it and struck the boy out. Every time. Every single time. The boy got a hit every now and again from other pitchers. Once he got a two-base hit. The ball went joyously through the air, bounced and went over the center-field fence. A clear, good two-base hit. But it was a relief pitcher. And whenever Grasshopper Smith was in the box, the boy struck out. He and Johann Sebastian Bach— they were full of dirty tricks. They were pretty stuck-up too. He hated them both.

Meanwhile, he had not replied to Mr. Olinsky's question, and Mr. Olinsky got up from the piano and stood beside him, looking at him, and saw that the boy's eyes were bright with frustration and disappointment because he was no good at baseball and no good at music either.

"Come and sit down a minute, boy," said Mr. Olinsky, and he led him over to a little wickerwork sofa.

Mr. Olinsky was in his sixties, and from the time he was this boy's age, he had given all his life to music. He loved the boy, though he had known him for only a year. He was a good boy, and he had a good ear. He wanted him to get excited about music, and the boy was not excited about it. He didn't practice properly. He didn't apply himself. There was something lacking, and it was up to him, Mr. Olinsky, to supply whatever it was that was lacking so that the boy would really enter into the magic world of music.

How to get to him then? How to make real contact with this American boy when he himself was, though a citizen, foreign-born?

He started to talk about his own youth. It had been a grim

youth in Petrograd. His parents were poor. His father had died when he was young, and his mother had, by a great struggle, got him into the conservatory. She had enough money for his tuition only. Eating was a problem. He could afford only one good meal a day at the conservatory cafeteria so that he was almost always hungry and cold. But he remembered how the great Glazunov had come to the cafeteria one day and had seen him with a bowl of soup and a piece of bread.

"This boy is thin," Glazunov had said. "From now on, he is to have two bowls of soup, and they are to be big bowls. I will pay the cost."

There had been help like that for him—occasional help coming quite unexpectedly—in those long, grinding, lonely years at the conservatory. But there were other terrible times. There was the time when he had reached such an age that he could no longer be boarded at the conservatory. He had to give up his bed to a smaller boy and find lodgings somewhere in the city.

He had enough money for lodging, but not enough for food. Always food. That was the great problem. To get money for food, he had taken a room in a house where the family had consumption. They rented him a room cheaply because nobody wanted to board with them. He would listen to the members of the family coughing at nighttime—the thin, shallow, persistent cough of the consumptive. He was terribly afraid—afraid that he would contract consumption himself, which was incurable in those days, and die. The thought of death frightened him. But he was equally frightened of disappointing his mother, for if he died he would not graduate, and all her efforts to make him a musician would be wasted.

Then there was the time he had had to leave Russia after the revolution. The awful standing in line to get a visa and then to get assigned to a train had taken seven months. And the train to Riga—what an ordeal that had been. Normally, it took eighteen hours. But this train took three weeks. Three weeks in cattle cars in midwinter, jammed up against his fellow passengers, desperately trying to save his violin from being crushed. A baby had died in the cattle car, and the mother kept pretending it was only asleep. They had had to take it from her by force eventually and bury it beside the tracks out in the howling loneliness of the countryside.

And out of all this, he had gotten music. He had become a musician. Not a concert violinist, but a great orchestral violinist, devoted to his art.

He told the boy about this, hoping to get him to understand what he himself had gone through in order to become a musician. But when he was finished, he knew he had not reached the boy.

This is because he is an American boy, Mr. Olinsky thought. *He thinks all these things happened to me because I am a foreigner, and these things don't happen in America. And maybe they don't. But can't he understand that if he made all these efforts to achieve music—to be able to play the works of Johann Sebastian Bach as Bach wrote them—it is surely worth a little effort on his part?*

But it was no good. The boy, he knew, sympathized with him. But he had not made real contact with him. He hadn't found the missing something that separated this boy from him and the boy from music.

He tried again. "Tell me," he said, "what do you do with your day?"

"I go to school," said the boy flatly.

"But after that? Life is not all school."

"I play ball."

"What kind of ball?" asked Mr. Olinsky. "Bouncing a ball against a wall?"

"No," said the boy. "Baseball."

"Ah," said Mr. Olinsky. "Baseball." And he sighed. He had been more than thirty years in the United States, and he didn't know anything about baseball. It was an activity beneath his notice. When he had any spare time, he went to a concert. Or sometimes he played chess. "And how do you do at baseball?" he said.

"Oh—not very good. That Grasshopper Smith. He always strikes me out."

"You have a big match coming up soon perhaps?"

"A game. Yes. Tomorrow. The Giants against the Yankees. I'm on the Yankees. It's the play-off. We are both tied for first place." For a moment he seemed excited, and then he caught a glimpse of the great musicians around the wall and the bleak stare of Johann Sebastian Bach, and his voice went dull again. "It doesn't matter," he said. "I'll be struck out."

"But that is not the way to think about it," said Mr. Olinsky. "Is it inevitable that you be struck out? Surely that cannot be so. When I was a boy—" Then he stopped, because when he was a boy, he had never played anything remotely approaching baseball, and so he had nothing to offer the boy to encourage him.

Here was the missing part then—the thing that was missing between him and the boy and the thing that was missing between the boy and Johann Sebastian Bach. Baseball. It was just something they didn't have in common, and so they couldn't communicate with each other.

"When is this game?" said Mr. Olinsky.

"Three in the afternoon," said the boy.

"And this Grasshopper Smith is your *bête noire*—your black beast, huh?"

"Yeah," said the boy. "And he'll be pitching. They've been saving him for this game."

Mr. Olinsky sighed. This was a long ways from "The Arioso." "Well," he said, "we will consider the lesson over. Do your practice, and we will try again next week."

The boy left, conscious that all the musicians were watching him. When he had gone, Mr. Olinsky stood before the portrait of Johann Sebastian Bach.

"Baseball, Maestro," he said. "Baseball. That is what stands between him and you and him and me. You had twenty children, and I had none. But I am positive that neither of us knows anything about baseball."

He thought about this for a moment. Then he said, "Twenty children—many of them boys. Is it possible, Maestro—is it just possible that with twenty children and many of them boys . . . ? You will forgive the thought, but is it just possible that you may have played something like baseball with them sometimes? And perhaps one of those boys always being—what did he say?—struck out?"

He looked hard at the blocky features of Johann Sebastian Bach, and it seemed to him that in one corner of the grim mouth there was a touch of a smile.

Mr. Olinsky was late getting to the Clark Recreation Park for the play-off between the Giants and the Yankees because he had spent the morning transposing "The Arioso" from A major into C major to make it simpler for the boy. Indeed, when he got there, the game was in the sixth and last inning, and the score was three to nothing in favor of the Giants.

The Yankees were at bat, and it seemed that a moment of crisis had been reached.

"What's happening?" Mr. Olinsky asked a man seated next to him who was eating a hot dog in ferocious bites.

"You blind or something?" asked the man. "Bases loaded, two away, and if they don't get a hitter to bring those three home, it's good-bye for the Yankees. And look who's coming up to bat. That dodo!"

Mr. Olinsky looked and saw the boy walking to the plate.

Outside the studio and in his baseball uniform, he looked

very small. He also looked frightened, and Mr. Olinsky looked savagely at the man who had called the boy a dodo and was eating the hot dog, and he said the only American expression of contempt he had learned in all his years in the United States: "You don't know nothing from nothing," Mr. Olinsky snapped.

"That so?" said the hot-dog man. "Well, you watch. Three straight pitches and Grasshopper will have him out. I think I'll go home. I got a pain."

But he didn't go home. He stayed there while Grasshopper looked carefully around the bases and then, leaning forward with the ball clasped before him, he glared intently at the boy. He pumped twice and threw the ball. The boy swung at it and missed, and the umpire yelled, "Strike one."

"Two more like that, Grasshopper," yelled somebody. "Just two more and it's in the bag."

The boy turned around to look at the crowd and passed his tongue over his lips. He looked directly at where Mr. Olinsky was sitting, but the music teacher was sure the boy had not seen him. His face was white and his eyes glazed so that he didn't seem to be seeing anybody.

Mr. Olinsky knew that look. He had seen it often enough in the studio when the boy had made an error and knew that however much he tried, he would make the same error over and over again. It was a look of pure misery—a fervent desire to get an ordeal over with.

The boy turned again, and Grasshopper threw suddenly

and savagely to third base. But the runner got back on the sack in time, and there was a sigh of relief from the crowd.

Again came the cool examination of the bases and the calculated stare at the boy at the plate. And again the pitch with the curious whip of the arm and the release of the ball one second later. Once more the boy swung and missed, and the umpire called, "Strike two." There was a groan from the crowd.

"O and two the count," said the scorekeeper, but Mr. Olinsky had risen from the bench and, pushing his way between the people on the bleachers before him, he went to the backstop fence.

"You," he shouted to the umpire. "I want to talk to that boy there."

The boy heard his voice and turned and looked at him aghast. "Please, Mr. Olinsky," he said. "I can't talk to you now."

"Get away from the back fence," snapped the umpire.

"I insist on talking to that boy," said Mr. Olinsky. "It is very important. It is about Johann Sebastian Bach."

"Please go away," said the boy, and he was close to tears. The umpire called for time-out while he got rid of this madman, and the boy went to the netting of the backstop.

"You are forgetting about 'The Arioso'!" said Mr. Olinsky urgently. "Now, you listen to me, because I know what I am talking about. You are thinking of a quarter note, and it should be five sixteenths. It is a quarter note—C sharp—held for one sixteenth more. *Then* strike. You are too early. It must be exactly on time."

"What the heck's he talking about?" asked the coach, who had just come up.

The boy didn't answer right away. He was looking at Mr. Olinsky as if he had realized for the first time something very important he had been told over and over again, but had not grasped previously.

"He's talking about Johann Sebastian Bach," he said to the coach. "Five sixteenths. Not a quarter note."

"Bach had twenty children," said Mr. Olinsky to the coach. "Many of them were boys. He would know about these things."

"For land's sake, let's get on with the game," said the coach.

Mr. Olinsky did not go back to the bleachers. He remained behind the backstop and waited for the ceremony of the base inspection and the hard stare by the pitcher. He saw Grasshopper pump twice, saw his hand go back behind his head, saw the curiously delayed flick of the ball, watched it speed to the boy, and then he heard a sound that afterward he thought was among the most beautiful and satisfying he had heard in all music.

It was a clean, sharp *click*, sweet as birdsong.

The ball soared higher and higher into the air in a graceful parabola. It was fifteen feet over the center fielder's head, and it cleared the fence by a good four feet.

Pandemonium broke loose. People were running all over the field, and the boy was chased around the bases by half his teammates, and when he got to home plate he was thumped upon the back and his hair ruffled, and in all this Mr. Olinsky caught one glimpse of the boy's face, laughing and yet with tears pouring down his cheeks.

A week later, the boy turned up at Mr. Olinsky's studio for his violin lesson. He looked around at all the great musicians on the wall, and they no longer seemed to be disapproving and disappointed in him.

Paganini was almost kindly. There was a suggestion of a chuckle on the noble profile of Mozart, and Beethoven no longer looked so forbidding. The boy looked at the portrait of Johann Sebastian Bach last.

He looked for a long time at the picture, and then he said two words out loud—words that brought lasting happiness to Mr. Olinsky. The words were, "Thanks, Coach."

"The Arioso" went excellently from then on.

Leonard Wibberley

The Old Refrain

$\mathcal{F}$ritz Kreisler, the violinist, found himself in Hamburg one evening with an hour to spare before taking his boat to London where he was to play the following evening. So he wandered into a music shop.

The proprietor asked to see his violin, which he always carried under his arm. In a moment he disappeared, to reappear with two policemen. One laid his hand on Kreisler's shoulder and said, "You are under arrest."

"For what?" asked Kreisler in disbelief.

"You have Fritz Kreisler's violin."

"Well, I *am* Fritz Kreisler."

"Come, come," said the policeman, "you cannot pull that one on us. Come to the station."

Kreisler's boat sailed in an hour. He had to do some quick thinking.

He looked around, and in the corner he saw a Victrola. Kreisler asked the proprietor if he had any of Fritz Kreisler's records. He produced "The Old Refrain," put it on, and played it through.

"Now," Kreisler said, "let me have my violin." Then, with

whatever skill he could command, he played "The Old Refrain." When Kreisler was through, he asked, "Are you satisfied now?"

With profuse apologies, they bowed him out to freedom.

Sometimes when life's masters are in our very presence, we don't recognize them. Perhaps, we have grown a bit farsighted in our living. We look *out there* for the wonders of life when all the time God's wonders are *in here*. Searching for his glories begins in your own heart.

The Great Pretender

*O*ne of the things I've enjoyed doing through the years is writing plays and musicals to be enacted for the church. Not really being a playwright, I can honestly say that some of them have been fair and the rest have been disposable.

In the early 1970s I came up with a scheme for our church to act out stories from the Bible for our Vacation Bible School. In the process of putting it together, we recruited eight couples in the church to prepare one minidrama of a Bible story to be presented to the children. They had to find their own players, decorate their rooms, write their own dramas, make their own costumes—the works.

The children were divided into "tribes" by age group and led by adults. Each tribe saw two Bible stories each night for four nights, moving from room to room as necessary. On the last night of VBS, everyone came to the final-night drama in the church auditorium.

One of the couples who agreed to prepare a minidrama was assigned the story of Jesus driving the money-changers out of the temple. And they did a magnificent job of decorating their room with a mural of the columns of the temple all around three walls of the room. Their drama was also well written and rehearsed.

In finding actors for their story, they asked one of their friends to play the role of Jesus. He was a big, burly kind of guy that drove a cross-country truck, chewed tobacco, and hit home runs on the softball team. However, he rarely made it to the church services or participated in the more spiritual aspects of church life. And his personal relationship with the Man he was to play was definitely limited to a nodding acquaintance.

When they first asked him to get involved in the drama, Rick (not his real name) declined, saying, "That's just not my bag." However, after some arm twisting and the wife's bribing him with her award-winning chili, he reluctantly agreed.

The first time I saw Rick in his Jesus costume, I almost laughed in his face because it seemed so out of character for him. Still, at that point, he appeared to be taking his job quite seriously; so I contained myself and congratulated him on his *unusual* interpretation of the role.

When VBS week finally arrived, Rick played his role to the hilt, yelling at the money-changers to "Git outta here!" (We were in the South, you see.) "You cain't turn my Father's house inta a den a'thieves, ya hear? So, jist git on out, and don't chew come back . . . evah!" Then he proceeded to destroy the temple by throwing over the tables of the money-changers (he actually enjoyed this part) and tossing the crooks out into the street. It was sort of a *Miami Vice*–like version of the story . . . but the kids got the point.

As planned, twice every night for four nights Rick donned his Jesus suit and cleansed the temple of insincere people. And the children loved it! They voted this story to be one of the best of the whole week.

The best part of the story, though, came *after* VBS. Somehow, *acting* like Jesus for several weeks had a lasting effect on Rick. He began coming to the church services a little more often. He even started coming to the midweek Bible study and staying for fellowship events. But the most powerful impact on him came from the young children at the church who, for weeks and months after VBS, would point at Rick and whisper, "Look! There's Jesus!"

Before long, the big, burly truckdriver no longer chewed tobacco, drank beer, or played hooky from church. He and his wife began team teaching Sunday-school classes, hosting youth activities, and leading teens on mission trips. He organized a youth softball team at the church and served as coach. And, after a few years, was chosen as a deacon to serve in the youth ministry. In short, he stopped *acting* like Jesus and began *living* like Jesus.

Oh, to Be Like Thee

Oh, to be like Thee! blessed Redeemer:

This is my constant longing and prayer;

Gladly I'll forfeit all of earth's treasures,

Jesus, Thy perfect likeness to wear.

Oh, to be like Thee! full of compassion,

Loving, forgiving, tender and kind,

Helping the helpless, cheering the fainting,

Seeking the wand'ring sinner to find.

Oh, to be like Thee! Lord, I am coming,

Now to receive th'anointing divine;

All that I am and have I am bringing;

Lord, from this moment all shall be Thine.

Chorus:

Oh, to be like Thee! Oh, to be like Thee!

Blessed Redeemer, pure as Thou art;

Come in Thy sweetness, come in Thy fullness;

Stamp Thine own image deep on my heart.

———

T. O. Chisholm

Driving Miss Myrtle

*O*ne day two older ladies were driving along through town on the way to their weekly card game at the senior citizens' center. They came to an intersection, and the traffic light was red, but Bertha just drove right through the light without slowing down. Myrtle looked over at Bertha, but she seemed perfectly calm and in control; so Myrtle thought, *Well, I thought that light was red, but perhaps I was mistaken.*

At the next intersection Bertha ran the red light again, and Myrtle sat up a little straighter in her seat and looked over at her. Again, Bertha was placidly driving along as if nothing had happened, and Myrtle thought, *Well, now, I'm almost sure that light was red. I'd better pay closer attention from now on.*

At the third intersection Bertha went through the red light again, this time barely missing a car that was crossing their path on the green light. Myrtle couldn't take it anymore; so she said, "Bertha! Don't you realize you drove right through that red light back there? What's wrong with you anyway?"

Bertha, looking at Myrtle with a startled expression, said, "Am I driving?"

Originator Unknown

The Boy and the Bear

$\mathcal{I}$n the early pioneer days of our country, a boy and his family lived in the backwoods, far away from other people and villages. After they had lived there for some time, they heard that a school had been opened a few miles away. The family agreed that the boy should go to school.

The boy very much wanted to go to school where he could learn and meet some other children his own age. Still, part of the way to school led through a dense forest, and the boy was afraid. The boy's father was a strong, brave backwoodsman. He wanted his son to grow up to be strong and brave, too. So he told the boy that he would have to go to school alone.

Every day after that the boy walked through the dark forest to school. He was always afraid he would meet a bear or some wild Indians, but he kept going anyway. He enjoyed school, and he had made some good friends among the students.

As the days passed and he became more familiar with the woods, his fear began to melt away. He actually began to enjoy watching the birds and squirrels building their nests. He learned to whistle some of the birds' individual songs, and he knew where the rabbits lived in tree trunks and holes.

Then one afternoon, as he was walking along and whistling the redbird's song, a great grizzly bear came roaring out of the woods and rose up on its hind feet, clawing the air and growling ferociously. The boy froze with fear. He couldn't cry out. He couldn't run. He was simply frozen in terror. Even if he had been able to run, it would have done no good, because the bear could have easily caught him.

The bear and the boy stood facing each other for several seconds, the boy's eyes wide with horror, and the bear's fangs bared and dripping with angry slobber. It seemed like an eternity for the boy. Then, suddenly, a shot rang out! And the bear collapsed on the ground . . . dead. And the boy slowly sank to the ground, sobbing with relief and looking around to see who had saved him.

From the bushes nearby the boy's father emerged. "It's all right, son. The bear's dead. He can't hurt you now." And he reached down and pulled his son into his big, strong arms of protection.

"Father, where did you come from? How were you here at just the right minute?"

"I've been with you all the time, son," smiled the father. "Every morning I've followed you to school, and every afternoon I've been in the shadows watching you, making sure you were safe."

"But father, why didn't you tell me you were there? I would not have been afraid if I'd know you were there."

"I kept myself hidden from you, son, because I wanted you to learn to be brave. And you have," smiled the father. "I'm very proud of you."

We, too, can be brave in this dark world, because our Father has said, "Fear not; I am with you."

———

Adapted from O. Osborn Gregory,

The Methodist Recorder

A Wendy Story

$\mathcal{W}$endy Stoker, age nineteen, was a freshman athlete at
the University of Florida. She placed third, just 2.5 points
from first place, in the Iowa girls' state diving championship.
She worked two hours a day for four years to get there.

Later, at the University of Florida, she worked twice as
hard to earn the number-two position on the varsity diving
squad. She was aiming for the national finals.

At the time, Wendy carried a full academic load, found
time for bowling, and was an accomplished water-skier. But
perhaps the most remarkable thing about Wendy Stoker was
her typing. She banged out forty-five words per minute on
her typewriter . . . with her toes!

Oh, did I forget to mention that Wendy was born without
arms?

Art Linkletter

Oops!

$\mathscr{A}$ man opened a new business, and his best friend sent him a floral arrangement. The friend dropped in a few days later to visit his buddy and was pained to see that the flowers had a sign that read, "Rest in peace."

He called the florist to complain. Realizing the cards had been switched, the florist said, "It could be worse. Somewhere in the city is an arrangement in a cemetery that reads, 'Congratulations on your new location.'"

———

Charles R. Swindoll
Tale of the Tardy Oxcart

A Worthy Cause

$\mathcal{A}$utomaker Henry Ford once went on vacation to Dublin, Ireland. While there he visited an orphanage where they were preparing to construct a new building. When the director of the building fund heard that Mr. Ford had visited the orphanage, he decided to call on the famous and wealthy man to ask for a donation.

After their visit, Ford decided to make a donation to the worthy cause; so he gave the man a check on the spot for two thousand pounds, which was quite a gift in those days. Ford's generosity was so astounding that the news of it made the headlines of the local newspaper. Unfortunately, his gift was reported to be twenty thousand pounds, rather than two thousand.

The director of the orphanage called Henry Ford immediately to apologize for the misprint. He promised to call the paper right away and have a correction printed. But, feeling a little guilty about his generosity being so overblown, Ford said no. Instead, he took out his checkbook and wrote another check for eighteen thousand pounds and gave it to the director.

With the check Ford made one request, "When the new building opens, I want this inscription put on it: 'I WAS A STRANGER AND YOU TOOK ME IN.'"

A Warm Welcome

W hen Czar Nicholas ruled Russia, he decided to test the hospitality of his people to strangers. Against the advice of his family and administrators, he dressed himself in beggar's clothing and went out into the countryside. For an entire day he went from door to door, asking for food and shelter. He was refused by most and cursed at by many as they slammed their doors in his face.

Finally, at twilight and as it began to get cold, he knocked on the door of a humble cottage of an old peasant and his wife. The peasant was extremely poor, and his wife was ill. Still, he invited the beggar inside.

"We have little," said the peasant, "but what we have, we'll share with you."

The peasant gave the Czar a small amount of warm, wholesome food. Then he prepared a sleeping mat for him on the floor near the fire, with apologies that the mat was the best he could do. They all settled down at last for the night.

When the peasant arose early the next morning to prepare the remainder of their food for themselves and the beggar, he found that the beggar had disappeared. He looked all around, but to no avail. So he went back inside to care for his wife.

Late in the afternoon of the next day, as the peasant and his sickly wife sat on the porch of their small cottage enjoying the warm sunshine, they saw a group of soldiers marching down the road toward their cottage. Behind the soldiers was a beautiful carriage, drawn by four magnificent horses.

"Oh, wife!" exclaimed the peasant. "What have I done? The soldiers must be coming to arrest me!"

"Halt!" shouted the captain of the guard. And the soldiers stopped short. "Right face!" And the soldiers turned sharply to face the peasant's little cottage.

Then the beautiful carriage drew up at the end of the walkway and stopped. The captain of the guard hurried to open the carriage door, and the soldiers all snapped to attention as Czar Nicholas stepped down from the royal carriage. Smiling graciously, he bowed to the peasant and his wife and greeted them warmly.

Suddenly the peasant's fears turned to joy as the Czar told them that it was he who, the night before, had been welcomed into their cottage as a beggar. Then he showered them with rich rewards—so many, in fact, that they never had to work or worry again.

Love and hospitality always bring great rewards.

———

Retold from Russian history

The Owl and the Pelican

*M*y wife has a weakness for books, especially old, choice religious books which are now out of print. At one time Foyles' in London had a large secondhand religious book department.

One day during the 1954 London Crusade, she was browsing through the books in Foyles' when a very agitated clerk popped out from behind the stacks and asked if she was Mrs. Graham. When she told him that she was, he began to tell her a story of confusion, despair, and frustration. His marriage was on the rocks, his home was breaking up, and business problems were mounting. He explained that he had explored every avenue for help and, as a last resort, planned to attend the services at Harringay Arena that night. Ruth assured him that she would pray for him, and she did. That was in 1954.

In 1955 we returned to London. Again my wife went into Foyles' secondhand book department. This time the same clerk appeared from behind the stacks, his face wreathed in smiles. After expressing how happy he was to see her again, he explained that he had gone to Harringay that night in

1954 as he had said he would, that he had found the Savior, and that the problems in his life had sorted themselves out.

Then he asked Ruth if she would be interested in knowing what verse it was that spoke to him. She was. Again he disappeared behind all the books and reappeared with a worn Bible in his hand. He turned to Psalm 102, which I had read the night that he had attended the Crusade. He pointed out verse 6, "I am like a pelican of the wilderness: I am like an owl of the desert." This had so perfectly described to him his condition that he realized for the first time how completely God understood and cared. As a result he was soundly converted to the Lord Jesus Christ. And, subsequently, so was his entire family.

My wife was in London during 1972 at the time of a Harringay reunion. As the ceremonies closed, a gentleman came up to speak to her, but he didn't have to introduce himself. She recognized the clerk from Foyles'. He was radiantly happy, introduced his Christian family, and explained how they were all now in the Lord's work—all because God spoke to him when he was "an owl of the desert"!

How graciously God speaks to us in our need . . . often through some obscure passage.

Billy Graham

Unto the Hills

I Choose Love

I choose love . . .

No occasion justifies hatred; no injustice warrants bitterness. I choose love. Today I will love God and what God loves.

I choose joy . . .

I will invite my God to be the God of circumstance.

I choose peace . . .

I will live forgiven. I will forgive so that I may live.

I choose patience . . .

I will overlook the inconveniences of the world. Instead of cursing the one who takes my place, I'll invite him to do so.

I choose kindness . . .

I will be kind to the poor, for they are alone. Kind to the rich, for they are afraid. And kind to the unkind, for such is how God has treated me.

I choose goodness . . .

I will go without a dollar before I take a dishonest one.

I choose faithfulness . . .

Today I will keep my promises.

I choose gentleness . . .

Nothing is won by force. I choose to be gentle.

I choose self-control . . .

I refuse to let what will rot rule the eternal . . . I will be drunk only by joy.

———

Max Lucado

When God Whispers Your Name

Dance on Wounded Feet

$\mathcal{R}$ichard Rumbren was arrested by the Communists in Romania many years ago because he believed in Jesus. For fourteen years, he and some other Christians were kept in one little room some thirty feet below the ground. And in all those years all they had was one little light bulb. It was a horrible life.

When he was finally released, Richard wrote a book titled Tortured for Christ to relate what he went through. And he began traveling about telling his story. But Richard could no longer stand up. His feet were so damaged by torture that he has to sit down to speak.

After the Wall came down in 1992, Richard got to go back to Romania. And they took him to show him the very first Christian bookstore in that nation. They were giving him the tour and showing him the books.

Then the owner said, "Come down stairs and see all the wonderful things we have in the warehouse."

So Richard and his elderly wife went down the stairs, and when they got to the room, Richard was shocked. Then everyone was startled when this old man with battered feet started dancing across the room.

"Richard, what's gotten into you?" asked the owner.

But he just started laughing and said, "This is the room they kept me in for fourteen years."

God had the last laugh. Nothing is too hard for him.

———

As told by Richard Rumbren

His "Innymunt"

$\mathcal{M}$r. Rogers was thinking. His thoughts went back twenty years, and he saw himself a young man doing a prosperous business, and although not in partnership, still intimately associated with one who had been his playmate, neighbor, and close friend for years. And then Mr. Rogers saw the financial trouble that had come upon him, and he thought bitterly that, if the friend had played the part of a friend, it might have been averted.

He saw the twenty years of estrangement and felt again the bitterness of that hour.

Mr. Rogers rose from his chair, and going to his safe, drew from it three notes for five thousand dollars each, due on the following Monday.

Twenty years is a long time to wait for justice, said he to himself, *but now, and without my lifting a finger, these notes have come into my possession, and I know, Robert Harris, that it will be hard work for you to pay them. I knew justice would be done at last.*

Mr. Rogers replaced the notes in his safe, and closing his office, went home to dinner.

Many a man will cry out for justice when it is revenge he desires.

On Monday morning, Mr. Rogers went to the station to take the eight o'clock train for Boston. He had just taken his seat when he heard his name spoken and saw Mr. Palmer, his neighbor, standing by his side.

"Are you going to town?" asked Mr. Palmer.

"Yes," was the reply. "Anything I can do for you?"

"I wish you would take charge of my little girl as far as the next station. Her grandmother will meet her there. I have promised her this visit for a week and had intended to take her down myself, but just at the last minute I received a dispatch that I must be here to meet some men who are coming out on the next train."

"Why, of course I will," said Mr. Rogers heartily. "Where is she?"

At these words, a tiny figure clambered onto the seat, and a cheerful voice answered, "Here I am!"

"Thank you," said Mr. Palmer. "Good-bye, Betty; be a good girl, and Papa will come for you tomorrow."

"Good-bye, Papa; give my love to the baa-lammie and all the west of the fam'ly," replied Betty.

People looked around and laughed at Betty's putting the lamb at the head of the family. They saw a very little girl under an immense hat, with a pair of big blue eyes and rosy cheeks.

Mr. Rogers put her next to the window and began to talk with her.

"How old are you, Betty?" he asked.

"I'm half past four; how old are you?" promptly returned Betty.

"Not quite a hundred," laughed Mr. Rogers, "but pretty old for all that."

"Is that what made the fur all come off the top of your head?" she asked, looking thoughtfully at his baldness, for the heat had caused him to take off his hat.

Mr. Rogers said he guessed so.

Betty pointed out various objects of interest and made original comments upon them, not at all abashed by her companion's age and gravity.

Suddenly she looked up and said, "I go to Sunday school."

"Do you? And what do you do there?"

"Well, I sing and learn a verse. My teacher gave me a new one 'bout bears, but I don't know it yet, but I know the first one I had. Want me to tell it to you?" The big blue eyes looked confidingly up at Mr. Rogers.

"Why, of course I do, Betty," he replied.

Betty folded her hands, and with her eyes fixed on her listener's face, said, "Love your innymunts."

Mr. Rogers flushed, and involuntarily put his hand on his pocketbook; but Betty, all unconscious of his thought, said, "Do you want me to 'splain it?"

The listener nodded, and the child went on: "Do you know what an innymunt is?" Receiving no answer, she said, "When anybody does naughty things and bweaks your playthings, he's an innymunt . . . Wobbie Fwench was my innymunt; he bweaked my dolly's nose, and he sticked burrs in my baa-lammie's fur, and he said it wasn't baa-lammie, noffin' but just a lammie." The big eyes grew bigger as she recalled this last indignity.

Mr. Rogers looked deeply interested, and who could have helped it, looking at the earnest little face? Betty continued to "'splain."

"It doesn't mean," she said, "that you must let him bweak all your dolls' noses nor call your baa-lammie names, 'cause that's wicked; but last week Wobbie bweaked his bicycle, and next day all the boys were going to wace, and when I said my pwayers, I told the Lord I was glad Wobbie bwoke his bicycle. I was.

"But when I wanted to go to sleep, I feeled bad here," and Betty placed a tiny hand on her chest and drew a long breath. "But by and by, after much as a hour I guess, I thinked how naughty that was, and then I telled the Lord I was sorwy Wobbie had bweaked his bicycle and I would lend him mine part of the time, and then I feeled good and was asleep in a minute."

"And what about Robbie?" asked Mr. Rogers.

"Well," replied the child, "I guess if I keep on loving him, he won't be a innymunt much longer."

"I guess not either," said Mr. Rogers, giving his hand to help her down from the seat as the cars slacked speed and stopped at the station. He led Betty from the car and gave her into her grandmother's care.

"I hope she has not troubled you," said the lady, looking fondly at the child.

"On the contrary, madam, she has done me a world of good," said he sincerely as he raised his hat, and bidding Betty good-bye, he stepped back into the car.

Mr. Rogers resumed his seat and looked out of the window, but he did not see the trees, nor the green fields, nor even the peaceful river with its thousands of water lilies, like stars in the midnight sky.

Had he told the Lord that he was glad his "innymunt" had broken his bicycle and could not join in the race for wealth and position? When he came to put the question straight to his own soul, it certainly did look like it.

It was no use for him to say the notes were honestly due. He knew that he could afford to wait for the money and that if Robert Harris was forced to pay them at once, he would probably be ruined. He heard the sweet voice of the child saying, "Love your innymunt," and he said in his heart, using the old familiar name of his boyhood days: "Lord, I am sorry Rob has broken his bicycle. I'll lend him mine until he gets his mended."

Had the sun come out suddenly from behind a dark cloud? Mr. Rogers thought so, but it had really been shining its brightest all morning.

A boy came through the train with a great bunch of water lilies, calling, "Lilies, cent apiece, six for five."

"Here, boy!" called Mr. Rogers. "Where did those come from?"

"White Pond, Lily Cove," said the boy, eyeing Mr. Rogers with some perplexity. He had been a train boy for five years and had never known Mr. Rogers to buy anything but the *Journal*.

"What'll you take for the bunch?"

"Fifty cents," replied the boy promptly.

Mr. Rogers handed him the half dollar and took the fragrant lilies. "How do you get into the cove now?" he asked as the boy pocketed the money and was moving on.

"Get out 'n' shove her over the bar," replied the boy as he went on.

Mr. Rogers looked at the flowers with the streaks of pink on the outer petals, at the smooth pinkish-brown stems, and thought of the time forty years before when he and Rob, two barefooted urchins, had rowed across White Pond in a leaky boat, and by great exertion dragged and pushed it over the bar, and been back home at seven o'clock in the morning, with such a load of lilies as had never been seen in the village before. Yes, he remembered it, and Rob's mother was frying doughnuts when they got back, and she gave them six apiece. Oh, she knew what boys' appetites were! She had been dead for thirty years now.

Just then the cars glided into the station, and everybody rushed out of the train. Mr. Rogers followed in a kind of dream. He walked along until he came to Sudbury Street and stopped at a place where he read, "Robert Harris, Manufacturer of Steam and Gas Fittings."

He entered the building and, going up one flight of stairs, opened the door and entered a room fitted up as an office. A man sat at a desk, anxiously examining a pile of papers. He looked up as Mr. Rogers entered, stared at him as if he could not believe his eyes, and, without speaking, rose from his chair and offered a seat to his visitor.

Mr. Rogers broke the silence. "Rob," he said, holding out his hand, "these came from the cove where we used to go, and . . . and . . . I've come around to say that if you want to renew those notes that are due today, I am ready to do so, and . . . and . . ."

But Mr. Harris had sunk into a chair and, with his head in his hands, was sobbing as if his heart would break.

Mr. Rogers awkwardly laid the lilies on the desk and sat down. "Don't, Rob," he said at length.

"You wouldn't wonder at it, Tom," was the reply, "if you knew what I have endured for the past forty-eight hours. I can pay every penny if I have time, but to pay them today means absolute ruin."

"Well, I guess we can fix all that," said Mr. Rogers, looking intently into the crown of his hat. "Have you any more paper out?"

"Less than two hundred dollars," was the reply.

The twenty years of estrangement were forgotten like a troubled dream, and when they finally separated, with a clasp of the hand, each felt a dozen years younger.

"Ah!" said Mr. Rogers as he walked away with a light step. "Betty was right. If you love your innymunt, he won't be an innymunt any longer."

———

Author Unknown

... and in conclusion

$\mathcal{I}$t was Sunday morning, and my friend James was wrapping up his sermon of the day. He'd done an excellent job with his topic, he was thinking to himself, when the disruption occurred.

One of the older men in the church had been sitting about halfway back. He and his wife were parents of a tiny, two-year-old surprise package that had been divinely delivered to them late in life. The wife was out of town for a day or two, and the husband had spent the entire sermon trying to keep that little bundle of energy under reverent control.

Finally, just as James was ready to make his concluding point, the man could take no more. So he picked up the little girl and started out the back of the auditorium to apply some good old homemade discipline to the appropriate place. Walking out, he had his back to James, but the tot, being carried in typical over-the-shoulder fashion, was facing James.

Now, little Betsy was familiar with this exit routine and fully aware of its coming reward. So, just as the father pushed through the double swinging doors out of the auditorium, she threw out her arms to James and screamed in a plaintive wail, "Save me!"

The congregation erupted into stifled laughter, of course, and James later confessed that the rest of his sermon was strictly anticlimactic.

We could all take a lesson from Betsy, though. When you're up to your ears in trouble in this life, and it looks as if the worst is yet to come, don't be afraid to throw out your arms to God and call for help. He'll hear you, and he'll answer.

Mary Hollingsworth
A Few Hallelujahs for Your Ho Hums

Apache Prayer of Benediction

Traditional

Now you will feel no rain, for each of you
will be shelter to the other.
Now you will feel no cold, for each of you
will be warmth to the other.
Now there is no loneliness for you.
Now you are two persons, but there is only
one life before you.
Go now to your dwelling place,
to enter into the days of your togetherness,
And may your days be good,
and long together.

More! More!

*L*ieutenant Gitz Rice was a member of a famous Canadian regiment, which went to France in World War I. The regiment fought in Flanders' Fields. It fought across the desolate "No Man's Land" under cover of a fearsome barrage, and sometimes even without the protection of the sheltering shells.

Rice's company carried a strange implement of war with them—an old dilapidated piano. On that old piano in France, Gitz Rice composed one of the famous songs of the soldiers, "Mademoiselle from Armentieres."

The afternoon before Christmas Eve the Canadians decided that the piano should be taken up to the front-line trenches. It was hoisted into an army truck and finally deposited at its destination.

Forced peace had settled over "No Man's Land" that night, but the barbed wire remained, and a morning attack threatened each side. The hostile troops were so close that the Canadian soldiers could hear the Germans talking to each other.

Shortly before the hour of midnight, Rice began playing Christmas carols in the British trench. First he played, "Silent Night, Holy Night." This was followed by "Hark! The Herald Angels Sing" and other beloved carols familiar to all the Christian world.

The Canadian soldiers sang quietly at first, and then lustily. Then they paused, thinking they were hearing an echo from the surrounding hills. From across the shallow field they heard the German troops singing with them. It was Christmas Eve.

Rice then played an aria from Wagner's "Tannhäuser." As he began the opening chords, a Canadian soldier mounted the rim of the parapet and, in plain sight of the Germans, sang the words of the aria.

When the aria stopped, silence fell over the field. Then suddenly a cry broke out from the Germans: "More! More!" So one of their own singers, a rich baritone, repeated the song to Rice's accompaniment, standing silhouetted against the moonlight as a clear target for British rifles. And when it finished, the Canadians cheered and cried out, "More! More!"

No rifle fire was heard that Christmas Eve. No singer was shot. Hatred had, at least for that one heaven-touched night, melted into love in memory of One greater than any war or enemy. And when I look around at the hatred, distrust, and prejudice that poison our world today, I want to cry out for everyone to hear, "More! More!" More love. More hope.

More peace. More of the One who is greater than any war
or enemy.

———

From World War I Records

A Farewell Blessing

*W*hat would I give you, if it were within my power? I would pray a blessing for you on each of the twelve days of Christmas:

*O*ne faithful friend to help carry your load.

*T*wo cups of Christmas cheer—one to savor, one to share.

*Th*ree special gifts for you to give away—one to show love, one to make peace, and one to bring joy.

*F*our hours of quiet solitude in which to dream your fondest dreams for the coming year.

*F*ive glorious sunsets unmarred by clouds or crowds.

*S*ix happy songs to sing of Christmas warmth and gladness.

Seven golden threads to run through your life: faith, virtue, knowledge, patience, godliness, kindness, and love.

Eight precious memories of long ago to keep you forever young.

Nine words of hope to calm your troubled heart: *Jesus Christ is the same yesterday, today, and forever.*

Ten minutes of creativity at its height.

Eleven smiles from strangers to renew your faith in people.

Twelve tranquil months of peace and love.

May the Giver of all good gifts bless you with these today and always.

Bibliography

Adams, Abigail. "Placed by Providence." Public domain.

Ancker, Frances, and Cynthia Hope. "Last Day on Earth." Used by permission of the Toronto Star Syndicate.

Augsburger, David. *The Freedom of Forgiveness*. Chicago: Moody Press, 1970.

"A Warm Welcome." Retold from Russian history.

"A Worthy Cause." Written from facts in public domain.

Brock, Anita. *Divorce Recovery*. Fort Worth: Worthy Publishing, 1991. Used by author's permission.

Campolo, Anthony. *Who Switched the Price Tags?* Waco: Word Books, 1986.

Carroll, Lewis. *Alice's Adventures in Wonderland*. Public domain.

Chisholm, T. O. "Oh, to Be Like Thee," 1897.

Crosby, Fanny J. "Blessed Assurance," 1873.

Demcheshen, Michael Kit. "Abducted." Used by permission of Michael Demcheshen.

"Driving Miss Myrtle." Originator unknown.

Echols, Eldred. "Sam, the Garbage Man." Used by permission.

Engstrom, Ted. *The Pursuit of Excellence*. Grand Rapids: Zondervan Publishing House, 1982. Used by permission of Zondervan Publishing House.

_____. *Motivation to Last a Lifetime*. Grand Rapids: Zondervan Publishing House, 1984. Used by permission of Zondervan Publishing House.

Faulkner, Paul. *Making Things Right When Things Go Wrong*. Nashville: Word Publishing, 1986.

Galloway, Dale. *Rebuild Your Life*. Grand Rapids: Zondervan Publishing House, 1978.

"Gettin' Thar." *Cappers Weekly*. Saint Louis, Missouri.

Graham, Billy. *Unto the Hills*. Dallas: Word Publishing, 1996.

Gregory, O. Osborne. Chicago: *The Methodist Recorder*, 1942.

"Greyfriars Bobby." From Scottish history. Public domain.

"His 'Innymunt'." *The Youth's Instructor*, 1 December 1914.

Hollingsworth, Mary. *A Few Hallelujahs for Your Ho Hums*. Fort Worth: Brownlow, 1988. Used by permission of Shady Oaks Studio, Bedford, Tex.

_____. "Everything I Need to Know as a Woman I Learned from Lucille Ball," 1996. Used by permission of Shady Oaks Studio, Bedford, Tex.

_____. "The Hans Shroud Story." Written from facts in public war records.

_____. "I Pledge Allegiance." From public record facts presented in a speech by Captain John McCain.

_____. "The Last Petal," 1981. Used by permission of Shady Oaks Studio, Bedford, Tex.

_____. "Opportunity," 1989. Used by permission of Shady Oaks Studio, Bedford, Tex.

_____. *Rainbows*. Norwalk: C. R. Gibson Company, 1989. Used by permission of Shady Oaks Studio, Bedford, Tex.

Johnson, Barbara. *Living Somewhere Between Estrogen and Death*. Nashville: Word Publishing, 1997.

Josefowitz, Natasha. "The True Secret of Happiness." In *Too Wise to Want to be Young Again*. Boulder: Blue Mountain Press, 1992.

Larson, Bruce. *Believe and Belong*. Grand Rapids: Fleming H. Revell, a division of Baker Book House Company, 1982.

LeBoeuf, Michael. *How to Win Customers and Keep Them for Life*. Berkley: Berkley Publications Group, 1989.

Linkletter, Art. "A Wendy Story." Used by author's permission.

Lucado, Max. *In the Eye of the Storm*. Nashville: Word Publishing, 1991.

_____. *Just Like Jesus*. Nashville: Word Publishing, 1998.

_____. *When God Whispers Your Name*. Nashville: Word Publishing, 1994.

Manning, Brennan. *Abba's Child: The Cry of the Heart for Intimate Belonging*. Colorado Springs: NavPress, 1994.

McDowell, Josh, and Norm Geisler. *Love Is Always Right.* Nashville: Word Publishing, 1996.

"More! More!" Retold from World War I records.

Nelson, H. Lee. "I'll Be Seeing You." Used by permission.

Rosten, Leo. *Captain Newman, M.D.* New York: Harper & Row, 1961.

"Rules for Teachers," 1872. Public domain.

Rumbren, Richard. "Dance on Wounded Feet." Used by permission.

Ruskin, John. "My Wish for You." Public domain.

"The Secret." Public domain.

Selzer, Richard. *Mortal Lessons: Notes on the Art of Surgery.* Quoted in Max Anders, *30 Days to Understanding the Bible.* Dallas: Word Publishing, 1994.

Shrode, Clyde. "Speaking of Electricity." Used by permission.

Sproul, R. C. *In the Presence of God.* Nashville: Word Publishing, 1999.

Swindoll, Charles R. *Come Before Winter.* Nashville: Word Publishing, 1996.

_____. *Tale of the Tardy Oxcart.* Nashville: Word Publishing, 1998.

Tan, Paul Lee. *Encyclopedia of 7700 Illustrations.* Rockville: Assurance Publishers, 1979.

Truman, Harry S. "A Good Question." Public record.

Wibberley, Leonard. "The Captive Outfielder," *The Saturday Evening Post*, 25 March 1961.

Wilcox, Ella Wheeler. *Poems of Power*. Chicago: W. B. Conkey Company, 1901.

Young, M. Norvel, with Mary Hollingsworth. *Living Lights, Shining Stars*. West Monroe, La.: Howard Publishing, 1997.